The
Commercial Bank
of Scotland Limited

ESTABLISHED 1810

•

HEAD OFFICE

14 · George Street
EDINBURGH

General Manager: IAN W. MACDONALD

•

BRANCHES THROUGHOUT SCOTLAND
AND THREE OFFICES IN LONDON

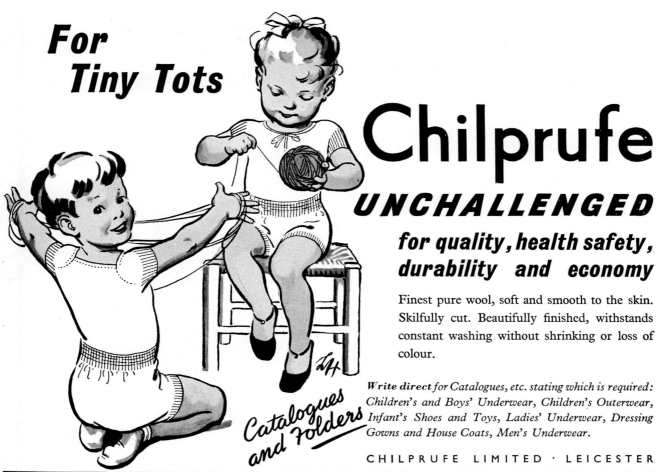

For Tiny Tots

Chilprufe
UNCHALLENGED

for quality, health safety, durability and economy

Finest pure wool, soft and smooth to the skin. Skilfully cut. Beautifully finished, withstands constant washing without shrinking or loss of colour.

Write direct for Catalogues, etc. stating which is required: Children's and Boys' Underwear, Children's Outerwear, Infant's Shoes and Toys, Ladies' Underwear, Dressing Gowns and House Coats, Men's Underwear.

Catalogues and Folders

CHILPRUFE LIMITED · LEICESTER

WISDOM'S DOUBLE CREAM SHERRY

Smooth to the palate—not too sweet, yet not too dry—every drop of this exquisite Sherry is sheer pleasure. Bottled in an attractive handy size bottle, Wisdom's Double Cream Sherry is available from licensed grocers.

RETAIL PRICE
28/6 per bottle
14/9 per half bottle

Bottled by
JAMES B. RINTOUL (Edinburgh) Ltd., EDINBURGH & GLASGOW

N° 5 - GARDENIA - CUIR DE RUSSIE - N° 22 - BOIS DES ILES

N° 5 CHANEL PARIS

THE MOST TREASURED NAME IN PERFUME

CHANEL

stop for
SUPER SHELL
and GO

SUPER SHELL with I.C.A.
gives you more GO for your money

The Standard Motor Company wish all owners and prospective owners

of their products a very happy Christmas

and a peaceful and prosperous New Year.

The Standard Motor Company Limited, Coventry, England.

"My Peggy is a young thing..."

ALLAN RAMSAY (1686-1758)

TIMES CHANGE. Today, the young Highland
lassie (unlike Allan Ramsay's sweetheart)
might well be found in the modern Philips
factory at Hamilton, working on the
manufacture of electric lamps or, maybe, the
famous 'Philishave' dry shaver, an occupation
which provides fulfilment for her quick,
skilful fingers: a friendly atmosphere that
often calls forth her sudden, elfin smile.

Traditional Scottish skill and pride in craftsmanship is ideally matched by Philips high standards
of manufacture — standards which have made
the name Philips renowned for dependability
in every continent of the world.

THE VAUXHALL VICTOR

Masterpiece of the creative engineer

The Victor stands supreme as the embodiment of all that is
modern in car design and construction. Elegant in appearance,
it combines comfort with high-performance, is easy to drive and,
above all, economical to maintain. You'll find all you could
wish for in the Victor, which you may inspect, test and buy at
any S.M.T. branch. Price £748, 7s. 0d. (including Purchase Tax).

AVAILABLE FOR EARLY DELIVERY

S.M.T. SALES & SERVICE COMPANY LIMITED

EDINBURGH, FALKIRK, GLASGOW, ABERDEEN, DUNDEE,
DUMFRIES, INVERNESS, KIRKCALDY, MUSSELBURGH,
PERTH, CARLISLE, PENRITH

We are the Main Dealers for Vauxhall Cars and Bedford Trucks

All under one roof

Rail tickets at station prices

•

Sea and air bookings

•

Hotel reservations

•

Passport and visa formalities

•

Currency exchange

•

Travellers' Cheques

•

Personal and baggage insurance

•

Shipping and forwarding

•

Holidays and Coach Tours

•

Party Travel arrangements

THOS. COOK & SON, LTD.

15–17 GORDON STREET, GLASGOW, C.1

HEAD OFFICE : BERKELEY STREET, LONDON, W.1.   BRANCHES EVERYWHERE

xvi

The Bay, Oban, Argyllshire

SCOTLAND
Land of History and Romance

Where else will you find such a variety of
beautiful scenery concentrated in such a small
area ? You can enjoy it all in comfort when
you travel by train.

SEE SCOTLAND IN COMFORT BY BRITISH RAILWAYS

Drambuie
the liqueur you prefer to be offered

A member of the MacKinnon clan blending rare herbs in the Isle of Skye during the eighteenth century, according to the secret recipe of Drambuie.

SCOTLAND'S MAGAZINE ANNUAL, 1958

LIFE AMONG THE SCOTS

Published by

SCOTLAND'S MAGAZINE

6-7 CASTLE TERRACE, EDINBURGH

Telephone : FOUntainbridge 5222-3-4
Telegrams : " Rodanrayle, Edinburgh "

1958

Text written by
ALASTAIR BORTHWICK

Price 8/6

Postage and packing 1/5 extra Home   1/4 extra Overseas

fashionable as a . . .

warm as a . . .

soft as a . . .

colourful as a . . .

light as a . . .

flattering as a . . .

luxurious as a . . .

practical as a . . .

Cashmere Sweater

from the range of

PETER SCOTT

fully fashioned

knitted sportswear

made in Scotland.

INTRODUCTION

*W*HEN *the war ended I began to contribute a column to* Scotland's Magazine. *It was a monthly commentary on the things I saw going on around me, and it ran for ten years. This book has grown from it. There is a leavening of new material, but most of the pieces printed here are drawn from the* Scotland's Magazine *files.*

I can claim without immodesty that most of it has weathered well. Not more than one paragraph in ten of the original columns has been used, and it is easy to set oneself up as a prophet if one picks, as I have done, only the times when one happens to have been right. The reader may take it, therefore, that although this book spreads itself over a decade it does fairly represent Scotland today. In the few cases where it does not (as, for example, during the post-war period of rationing) the paragraph carries the date when it was written and the sequence of events is clear.

This book is one man's view of Scotland during a particularly interesting decade of its history, written on the spot at the time. I hope you enjoy it.

A. B.

Scotland
for the beginner

Since the last war Scotland's tourist trade has grown beyond belief, and now a large number of Scots acquire at least part of their incomes through entertaining visitors from other countries. This group of American visitors is sightseeing in Edinburgh.

TOURISTS to Scotland must first know this about us : that there is not one Scotland, but three, each with its own way of life. They are Highlands, the Lowlands, and the cities; and to have a real understanding of the country they must know how this division came about.

Once upon a time, just over two hundred years ago, the Highlands and the Lowlands might have been a thousand years and a thousand miles apart. Not only did they live in completely different ways, but they did not even speak the same language. Geography lay at the root of it. The northern half of Scotland is extremely mountainous; and the " grain " of the mountains runs, roughly speaking, from east to west, drawing a series

of parallel barriers across the country. Even today, roads are scarce in the remoter districts. Two or three centuries ago they were very rare indeed, even in areas which bordered on the Lowlands. Anyone who felt like fighting the Highlanders found himself in a jumble of rock and heather, far from home, trying to get to grips with an invisible enemy who had guerilla warfare reduced to a fine art.

The British Government, apart from an occasional clash, decided to live and let live; and for many generations a blind eye was turned to the goings-on behind the mountains. Provided the Highland chiefs did not overstep the mark, and they were generally too busy fighting among themselves to be much of a nuisance, they were allowed to do pretty much as they liked. They kept to their native glens, making their own laws, fighting their own wars, and sallying forth only occasionally to lift Lowland cattle or cock a snook at the Government. The centuries rolled by leaving them untouched. Anthropologists today declare that two hundred years ago, when the rest of Scotland was beginning to think in terms of the steam engine and heavy industry, the Highlands were still living in the Bronze Age.

Remember this when you travel the Highlands today.

The Things that Help

WE in Scotland refuse to be surprised by the phenomenal growth of our tourist trade. It seems to us that the millions now pouring in each summer are no more than our due. After all, we have the history and the scenery, and we have some interesting sidelines as well.

There are, for example, what might be called the specialists, the people of Scottish descent who would still come to see the land of their fathers if it all looked like the back of a Lanarkshire coal-bing. As there are said to be 20,000,000 expatriate Scots or their descendants scattered about the world as distinct from the 5,000,000 who have stayed at home, this gives us a flying start.

Three of the things our visitors come to see : dramatic hills (Argyll); a Highland river (the Dee); and romantic old buildings (Tantallon Castle).

Above: visitors admiring the famous Queen's View of Loch Tummel in Perthshire. Right: a visitors' bus cruising along the shore of Loch Long, Argyllshire.

Then there is the matter of names, the magical " Mac " which conjures up pictures of clan battle in the minds of inoffensive Macdonalds and Macleods and Macphersons all the way from Singapore to Beverly, Mass. Sooner or later they feel the urge to see where their forebears raided the neighbours' cattle.

Add to these the small size of the country and the variety of scene it contains, and a successful tourist trade is unremarkable. All the trimmings are there. Millions who know nothing else of European verse do know about Robert Burns, Edinburgh Castle's profile is familiar everywhere, and astonishing numbers of foreigners can sing at least the first two lines of *Auld Lang Syne* and the last two of *Loch Lomond*. These things all help.

Still, success depends ultimately on having the goods once the customers are inside; and there, we feel complacently, we do have them ready to hand. Scotland is a small country with superlative scenery. It can be " done " after a fashion in two or three days, yet it is so packed with excellences that some find a lifetime not long enough.

That is why tourists come to visit us despite the fact that we are a little to one side of the beaten track which leads good Americans to Paris. The English discovered us long ago, but now the visitors are coming from Europe and from the other side of the Atlantic as well.

Not, mind you, that it surprises us. Not at all. The only wonder is they didn't come sooner.

IT is an article of faith with all good Scots that their system of education is the best in the world. They could be right. Though the lead we held in the early days has almost disappeared as other less favoured nations, such as the English, have caught up with us, we may still have our noses just in front.

Of course it depends upon what one calls education. Our conception of it is fairly narrowly based. We teach our children (up to a compulsory minimum age of fifteen) to read and write and count, appreciate their mother-tongue, pick up a foreign language or two, and dabble a little in science; and if they are not academically inclined we have many " practical " subjects; but we do not go in much for civics, or general knowledge, or background material of that sort.

This curriculum, taught with great thoroughness, is apt to make overseas comparisons misleading. My own youngster, for example, appears to be at least a year ahead of his American cousins until one realises that they are taught many more subjects than he is. They have quantity, he has the concentrated dose. I prefer our way, but many might disagree with me.

The aim of the Scottish teaching profession is that every teacher should be a university graduate; and although this ideal has taken some hard knocks lately (teachers are not to be had in sufficient numbers, and uncertificated men and women are being used as stop-gaps) Scotland still has a much higher percentage of university-trained teachers than has England.

Classes are bigger than they should be, but smaller than they were. The building of new schools was abandoned in favour of houses after the war, but a serious effort is now being made to catch up. The teacher shortage is acute, but less acute than it is in several other countries.

There is controversy in plenty, and for years a long-drawn-out howl for more pay has been coming from the teachers; but behind it the fact remains that children in Scotland do get the education they are fitted to absorb, and that lack of money need never prevent a Scots child completing its education, even at university level. State grants and private bequests between them ensure that the lad or lass of ability can be carried through to the limit of capacity.

New Words

ONE of the biggest pieces of educational research ever undertaken in Scotland was recently completed and published under the straight-forward but not very exciting title of *The Scottish Pupil's Spelling Book*. The book is the fruit of ten years' research, and labour so painstaking as to be almost preposterous. Nothing else quite like it has ever been done in this country before.

The object of the exercise was to discover which words should be taught in our primary schools, and when. Very young children have a whole world to become accustomed to, and their need for words grows with their experience. New words taught too soon are a nuisance. Taught too late they leave the child without the means of expressing itself. It seemed to teachers ten years ago that some digging ought to be done, that we should discover which words a child used at four, and five, and six years of age, and so be able to teach him how to spell them as he came to need them.

Scots at School

So the Research Council's Panel on Spelling got to work.

Its members soon found there was no easy answer. Obviously the most commonly used words ought to be taught first, but the only lists showing frequency of use were based on adults and not on children. They would have to begin at the beginning.

They made a list of the things which interested children—things like food, and shelter, and games, and home and so on, and from it devised a list of sixty-eight subjects on which Scottish children could be expected to write spontaneously, without help. Then they invited our primary schools to send in letters or stories on these subjects.

The daunting total of 90,000 came in. For various reasons, such as signs of adult help, 20,000 were rejected. That left 70,000 juvenile letters and essays for the researchers to get their teeth into. The task was enormous, because what they then set out to do was to make two lists for each of the five classes in our primary schools, one list showing how many times each word in the 70,000 entries was spelled correctly, and another showing how many times each was spelled incorrectly. A further sorting divided up the words among the original sixty-eight subjects. When the job was done they knew which words each age-group most commonly used on most subjects under the sun, and which ones gave them most difficulty.

There were many surprises. For example, it soon became evident that the very youngest children were trying to use difficult words like biscuit, and sandwich, and lemonade—words which the old spelling books never tried to teach them. Other results were not unexpected. For instance, many of the mistakes occurred with very simple words, especially when they were rattled off in phrases. Common examples here were " cuppytea ", and " he must of gone "; and past tenses gave a lot of trouble: large numbers cheerfully put down " kickt ", " walkt ".

The new book gets round these difficulties by teaching children to spell words as they come to use them, and by hammering away at the phrases which research has shown to be common points of weakness. It also teaches the spelling of past and present tenses side by side.

It will not, of course, teach children to spell. They have to do that for themselves. It may, however, make their task easier by making it seem more practical and urgent and interesting. I do not even know how important this piece of research has been, though I suspect it has been worth the labour lavished on it. Certainly it has been a whale of a job.

The Tattie Howkers

THE report of the committee on potato-lifting, issued by the Scottish Education Department, made it clear that the practice of employing school children to gather the potato harvest was likely to remain with us for years to come. The committee regretted, the committee urged, but the committee did not solve. It could not do so, because the problem was then insoluble, and still to some extent remains so.

The report presented both sides fairly. It was a bad thing, it said, to interrupt a child's education at any time, and especially so when the time was the first term of the school year, the term least affected by illness, sport and other activities. No child was allowed to spend more than three weeks in the potato fields, but as the different varieties of potato ripened at different times, the school curriculum was disrupted for at least six weeks. Furthermore, those who stayed at school became as unsettled as those who left. The general effect was that the term was half way to Christmas before it had properly begun.

On the other hand, Britain was a potato-eating country, the English half of which could not grow its own seed-potatoes properly. We in Scotland not only produced our own crop for eating, but supplied most of Britain with seed. Britain was already importing some potatoes, and if school children did not help with the lifting we should have to import more, with grave repercussions on our trade balance. The other difficulty was that the potato demands a great deal of labour for a few weeks of the year and very little labour for the rest, the result being that the normal labour supply could not possibly cope. A pool was needed for the peak period, and the only pools available were either the schools or machinery.

Setting the pros against the cons the committee declared, reluctantly, that " it is necessary to exempt children from attendance at school to assist in lifting the potato crop if the acreage devoted to this vital crop is not to be drastically curtailed. We are of opinion that the production of a harvester or harvesters capable of operating efficiently under Scottish conditions is the only feasible alternative."

So far no one has been able to invent such a machine. Many have tried and some have partially succeeded, but no one has made a machine which will work under all conditions on every type of ground at a price the farmer can pay. So we fall back on an expedient which was old when history began, and use children.

The report concluded with the statement that, in view of the great educational loss arising from the potato-lifting, the Government ought to encourage in every way possible the invention of an efficient harvester and to regard the matter as urgent and important.

This tells us nothing we did not know already, but what else could the committee say? The facts are unavoidable. Either someone invents a machine, or our children will have a high old time in the fields each autumn. Considering how much we spend on education, this is not very sensible. But it cannot be helped.

Scots at work

The Sea Harvest (1953)

MY friend the lobsterman earns his bread and butter by his creels, and his jam by pure luck. He made a killing on seagull's eggs after the war, when you could hardly walk the beach without trampling them and Billingsgate was paying 15s. a dozen. Then there was the small matter of the dismasted yacht he towed in, and the habit trawlers used to have of piling up on his doorstep. There is more money in the sea than ever came out of it, even today when eggs are off the ration, and a new bell-buoy has knocked the bottom out of the salvage business. This year it was the Coronation.

He has had a record summer, thanks to the high jinks on what he calls the neighbouring island of Britain. Winter lobsters fetch a high price, but the weather makes them hard to catch. Summer lobsters are easy and plentiful, but the price is poor. This summer the country has been so full of visitors and so addicted to banquets that he has been able to sell at winter prices ever since May—about 10s. for the average lobster instead of the usual 5s. or 6s. This confirms his faith in the monarchy and his belief that something, however unlikely, will always turn up if you trust to the ravens and have a beach at your door.

The thing which interests me is the versatile nature of his income and the way in which this man, a remote and allegedly simple islander, continues to profit by the appetites and errors of the mainland. He calls it luck, but I am beginning to wonder.

All round Scotland's coasts are the communities of fisherfolk busy with the harvests of the sea. Top: a lobsterman examines his catch in the northern islands. Above: a fisherman mending his nets on the pier of an Ayrshire harbour. Right: fingers bandaged to ensure a good grip of the slippery herring, this typical Scottish fisher-lassie guts the " silver darlings " at a Scottish port.

A woman of the roads. Once a sturdy and independent race in their own right, with a traditional occupation which gave them the name of "tinkers", the wandering folk of the Scottish roads are now becoming less numerous every year.

The People of the Roads

THERE are people who claim to find romance in the Scottish tinker, but I have never been able to see it myself. He trudges the roads with his raggle-taggle wife and brood of children, engaged in no business that is easily discernible apart from hawking in a small way; and neither in his dress, which is undistinguished, nor in his manner, which is sullen, is there any trace of romance.

I do not know what happens to old tinkers. Those on the roads are seldom over forty; and their brood, either through magic or non-stop production, invariably starts in the perambulator and ranges upwards to about fourteen. They have the unique distinction of being recognisable on sight for what they are. Even the youngest tinker child soon acquires the tough tinker look.

Others can sing hey for the open road, but not myself. The pleasures of sleeping in a ditch are much over-rated, and in any case tinkers have been an anachronism since aluminium pots killed the tinsmith's trade and the motor-car made away with horses. Most of those still in business trudge the traditional routes (each clan has its own, jealously guarded) from force of habit as much as anything else.

With the old sources of livelihood gone, the charm of the council house becomes more and more persuasive. The tinkers are vanishing, taking to the towns and becoming absorbed into the ordinary humdrum population.

I am all for nonconformists in any walk of life, but I shall shed no tears when the last tinker leaves the roads for good. Neither will anyone else who lives in the country districts of Scotland.

Portrait of Charles Faa Blyth, the Gipsy King, at his coronation in 1898. Yetholm, a mile from the English Border, was a headquarters for gipsies until comparatively recent years.

A typical tinkers' camp in the Highlands. The women cook over an open fire. The man works on metal pans—the traditional trade which has now almost died out.

The face of Scottish Industry; a steel worker in one of the great works of Scotland's industrial belt.

Women at Work

MY friend the factory manager is greatly struck by the ways of Scotswomen. He comes from England himself, and tells me has never met anything like them before. He is in a unique position to study them, because he and his two assistants have to cope with an all-female staff.

He starts with compliments. Scotswomen work harder, take a keener interest in their work, and are more loyal to the firm than their sisters south of the Border. They do these things because there is more fire to them altogether. Unfortunately this same characteristic makes them willing and indeed eager to argue the hind leg off a donkey at any time of the day and at all seasons of the year. He gets results, but finds it wearing.

" Look at it this way," he says. " You go to the average English girl in a factory and you say to her: ' This won't do, you know. This job you've let through is terrible. Get this firm a bad name it will, if we put things like that on the market.' And she'll say: ' Well, you know 'ow it is. Turning out 'undreds all day long. A bad 'un's bound to slip through.' She's easy about it, and doesn't much care. Say the same to a Scots girl, no matter how tough she is, and ten to one she'll put her head down on the bench and burst into tears. You have to watch, you know. I'd done it three times before it dawned on me there was so much pride going about."

And pride, strangely enough, is the difficulty. It is not so much pride in the job as pride in themselves. They are individualists, each building a little corner of work for herself and defending it fiercely against all comers. A rebuke from the manager may bring tears because the girl feels she has lost face, but the merest hint of criticism or interference from anyone else brings her storming to the manager with a complaint. This makes his life very complicated. The English girl, he says, wouldn't bother.

Women being women and Scots being Scots, the ideal is not to have a job of great responsibility or difficulty, but one which is different from anyone else's. You can then imagine yourself to be indispensable and boss about anyone who is sent to help you. As a result, the factory is not really a team, but a host of individuals who have worked out for themselves a complicated system of precedence. It tallies in almost no way with the manager's list and is based on an entirely female scale of values. Every girl knows exactly where she stands, takes orders from those higher up, and is autocratic to the point of insolence to everyone lower down.

For example, one of those standing highest on this unofficial list is a girl still in her teens whose job is considerably less important than many others in the factory. She wheels a trolley round the different departments and makes up the requirements of the customers by collecting goods, checking them from an order sheet, and wheeling them away. Men would regard this as very small beer. Not so women. Her job allows her to stick her nose in everywhere and tell almost anyone to hand her this or hand her that. And that is what counts.

Everyone in the hierarachy guards her place jealously. Groups combine only to guard some imagined privilege. For example, there is the matter of cleaning up, an operation which takes place every Friday. The various departments of the factory are not partitioned off, but lie side by side on the open floor. Each is responsible for its own mopping and cleaning. The manager tells me that he has never laid down the exact boundaries between department and department, yet boundaries of the most precise kind do exist in the minds of the women, and they are never crossed. There may be a crack in the concrete floor, a corner by a machine or a bench. Each department cleans (to take the case of the crack, which zig-zags all over the place) exactly up to the line. Thanks to the zig-zags this is a complicated business and takes much longer than a straight slosh over the edge would do; but each Friday both sides clean to the line, no more, no less. One must, you see, give nothing away.

Oddly enough, this sort of thing means a great deal to Scotland, because it is the chief reason why English and overseas firms set up factories here. It may sound illogical and rather pointless, but the basic fact is that these strange practices grow from pride and interest in the job. A girl who doesn't care is not going to trouble to become heated about it to that extent. These girls do care, and they are typical. Even the

A woman arc-welder at work in a Scottish factory.

lack of team-work is not a disadvantage. No women anywhere have any sense of team-work, but in this country they have pride, which brings the desire to establish their own little corners, which brings in its turn the odd scale of precedence. The wise manager can use that scale to his own ends, make it do what team-work ought to do, fit it to his programme of work.

My friend says he reckons he earns his salary. He sometimes thinks wistfully of working with men who would speak his language and think his way. Most of all he wishes women wouldn't argue so much. But he is glad he came to Scotland. The output of his factory is high; and there is, he says, never a dull moment.

Small Contract

A manufacturer of earth-moving equipment was showing me round his factory and painting a glowing picture of the public works we could build now that we had trucks capable of moving 50 tons at 35 m.p.h. up 1 in 3 gradients without a road to support them. Dams and irrigation schemes which had never been possible before were now practical propositions, he said.

" What about the Pyramids? " I asked, " Supposing you had to build the Great Pyramid today, how long would it take you? "

" The Great Pyramid? " He looked at me perfectly seriously. " But that would be a small contract. Let me see now."

He sat down on a tyre which would have made an excellent garden seat for a dozen people and produced his slide-rule.

" Let me see. How many men built it orginally? "

" Opinions vary," I said, " But the general idea seems to be that it took 100,000 men twenty years to do the job."

" Dear me." He seemed distressed at the inefficiency of it all. " Well, let's figure it out. Say a couple of million tons of rock, and say we had to shift it 25 miles. I don't think they had to shift it that far, but let's make it difficult. We'd work two shifts. . . ." He fiddled with the slide-rule. ". . . that's 9.6 trips a day. Say 320 cubic yards per day per machine. Multiply by 300 working days in the year. Hm. Yes. We could do the lot in a year with twenty machines and forty men."

These machines and others like them (they're made in Scotland, by the way) are beginning to have a big effect on the world.

The March of Steel

SCOTTISH heavy industry starts with steel, and a fairly healthy start it is. Others, notably shipbuilding and engineering, are bedevilled by wage demands and demarcation disputes, strikes threatened and actual, and thoroughly bad feeling between management and the unions. In steel, sweet reasonableness prevails. Everything is done by negotiation, with both sides talking the same language and a good deal of sense as well. Indeed, I had some difficulty in arranging a broadcast discussion from Colvilles recently because the union representative and the works manager taking part both wanted to say the same thing.

In a country torn by strikes there is no substantial difference of opinion in the steel industry. There has not been a steel strike in Scotland for seventy years.

Colvilles (who make nearly all the steel in Scotland) have spent over £20,000,000 on their new plant at Ravenscraig, and they are about to spend another £30,000,000 or so on it. They spend with confidence, knowing that their men's union, alone among all the British unions, reckons that the more their men produce the more they will earn.

I wish a few other people thought in the same way, especially the forty unions who cover the shipyard men. Speaking as an outsider who has interviewed many of the leaders, I should say they have no interest in production at all. They do not consider that to be their business. Their business is getting higher wages.

It is not a happy set-up, but even so the shipyards are spending their millions too. Most of them are reorganising, and four are equipping themselves to build the big new tankers, so big that they are not much smaller than the *Queen Mary*. The Clyde has a greater capacity than ever before. All it needs is industrial peace to enjoy it.

The shape of things to come at Ravenscraig, near Motherwell, where in 1957 Colvilles completed and opened a £22½ million project comprising coke ovens, blast furnace and steel-making plant.

The unloading of iron ore from ships' holds at Glasgow's Terminus Quay on the river Clyde is an operation now speeded by efficient modern machinery. These giant frames contain the gear which extracts ore from holds in record time.

Grangemouth, at the estuary of the river Forth, has been the scene of one of the most spectacular industrial developments. Now international shipping unloads at her quays. Timber and oil are among the chief imports.

At Clydebridge steelworks—owned by the Colville group of companies—a glowing ingot is taken from the soaking pit to the cogging mill. Colvilles make nearly all the steel in Scotland.

The Puffers

WITHOUT wishing to hurt any feelings down at Customshouse Quay, on Glasgow's river Clyde, I feel I must make it clear from the start that there are more glamorous vessels afloat than the puffers. Puffers lack *chic*. They are small, fat, and ungainly, consisting mainly of hold-space with an engine tacked on behind; and the heaviest of them does not weigh more than 90 tons. They are broad in the beam and dumpy; and their lines, as Mr. Flecker said long ago about something else, have a monstrous beauty like unto the hindquarters of an elephant.

Nevertheless I regard the puffers with affection and respect. Not only do they serve the most difficult coastline of Scotland and do a job no other ship can do, but they have produced a breed of seamen whose exploits in the past have been almost as peculiar as the vessels themselves. There is nothing like the puffers anywhere else in Britain, and nothing like the puffermen anywhere else in the world. I defy anyone to produce, in any place other than the west of Scotland, a vessel with a cargo of one steam road-roller and ten tons of cockleshells under command of a skipper with a name like the Wee Protestant or Jock the Wrecker.

One of the Highland lifeline of little boats—the puffers—at Rothesay. Puffers go in on the tide, become beached as the tide ebbs, and then unload their cargoes on to lorries with their own derricks. No other British ship can do this. No other British ship needs to. It is only on the Highland coast that harbours are scarce.

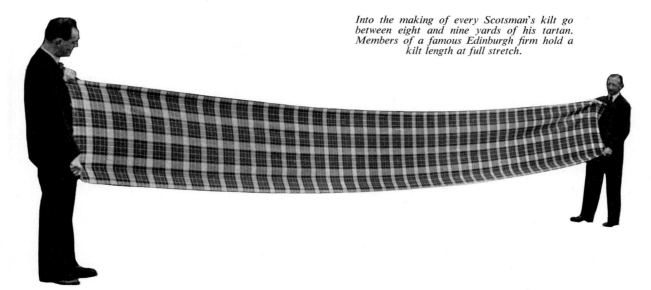

Into the making of every Scotsman's kilt go between eight and nine yards of his tartan. Members of a famous Edinburgh firm hold a kilt length at full stretch.

The Wearing of the Kilt

The kilt is much favoured by young Scots tramping the roads in summer.

THE experts disagree as to precisely when the kilt came to Scotland, but they are agreed as to how it came. The Celtic tribes which fought Caesar wore kilts of a kind, and when their drift north began, up through Cornwall, and Wales, and Ireland, they brought the kilt with them. A thousand years ago it was worn over large areas of Britain, and there was nothing specially Scottish about it. Only since the others stopped using it has it become the national dress of Scotland.

There are anything up to eight yards of cloth in a modern kilt, thickly pleated at the back and sides, with the pleats gathered at the waistband and swinging free below. No better walking dress exists. It is warm enough for winter, cool enough for summer, stands hours of rain before soaking, hangs well above the mud and the wet grass, and, thanks to the many thicknesses where the pleats are stitched at the small of the back, an excellent guard against the chills which rest after exercise can bring.

Also it is a dress with an air to it. If a man has the legs for it, it looks magnificent. Its Gaelic name is *feile beag*, or little kilt.

Its modern form is relatively new, for in the days of the clans it was the *breacan-feile*, or belted plaid, a much simpler garment. Then it was a sort of tartan blanket about two yards wide by five or six long. Part of

A family tartan is still something to be proud of, is still worn to good effect by those genuinely entitled to it. Above, a Highland family in the national dress that is also an everyday attire, at Portree in Skye. Kilts are not worn by women, for whom a tartan skirt of a longer and different cut is correct dress.

Kilt in the country (above) goes well with heather, bracken, the incomparable colour scheme of the Highlands, and the rugged lands that induce the long, swinging hillman's stride.

Guard at Edinburgh Castle. The kilt has been the coveted possession of some Scottish regiments since 1739.

it was wrapped round the body like a modern kilt, and the rest was flung over the shoulder and pinned there. You fought in it by day and used it as a blanket at night.

The kilt took a hard knock after the rebellion of 1745, when the wearing of the tartan was forbidden; and in the Highlands it has never since recovered. It is still worn by the Highland regiments, and it crops up in large numbers at city dances, where the Highland form of evening dress is popular; but it is no longer a workaday dress in the Highlands and has not been so for two centuries.

Its real home today is in the Youth Hostels, where its merits as a walking dress are recognised, and it is worn naturally. There it is found at week-ends and during the holidays, being worn where it was meant to be worn, on the hills and the heather.

Chief marshall of a recent Scottish motorists' hill climb was kilted Mr. Tom Forrest.

Hikers on a Loch Lomond pier, waiting for the boat which will take them to another of the little villages dotted round the loch.

The kilt in school; normal everyday wear in a Galloway schoolroom.

Kilt in the town—a splash of colour and a distinctive national flavour is brought to the grey of Scotland's First Street.

Scottish football attracts a large proportion of the energy and enthusiasm of the nation. The picture above shows the packed stadium at Ibrox, Glasgow, on the day of a big event.

Scots at Play

Scottish Football

SCOTTISH football is a very odd business. Not only are anything up to 100,000 people prepared to gather in one place to see twenty-two other people kick a ball (making as they do so a roaring sound unique in nature), but some of them become so inflamed by the spectacle that they fight for the honour of their team with anyone who happens to be handy. They appear to find a semi-religious satisfaction in this. Others, a shade more temperate, band themselves together into supporters' clubs and travel the country singing curious songs. Others again content themselves with arguments about the game, the players and the referee, and spend their leisure reading endless columns about the sport in the press. The most famous man in Scotland is Charlie Tully.

Now most of this is exactly as it should be. One cannot worry about atom bombs all the time, and the football clubs provide thousands of people with a harmless hobby which gives them something to look forward to and provides a little colour in life. The only trouble is that some people are taking it too seriously. For many years we have been treated to the spectacle of supporters being segregated at opposite ends of the ground in the interests of public safety when Rangers play Celtic; and recently the police courts on Monday morning have been filled with gentry who have tried to reinforce Saturday's argument with broken bottles and bicycle chains. What goes on in the rather dim brains of these people is difficult to imagine, but it seems to be an odd mixture of hero-worship, religious intolerance, mental deficiency, and the contents of the bottles they use so freely.

There are enough of them now to cause the magistrates serious concern, and the magistrates have been wondering what to do about it. Once, after long deliberation, they recommended that the most famous and acrimonious match of all, the New Year's Day Rangers-Celtic game, should no longer take place. Shrieks of fury arose on all sides and the Scottish Football Association refused flatly to cancel the match, their argument being that the misbehaviour of a few should not prevent the enjoyment of tens of thousands at the most popular game of the year, and that the magistrates had powers to deal with offenders and ought to use them more stringently.

Where I do part company with the Football Association is in their attitude to mid-week games, which is the other thorny point. A mid-week

cup-tie in Glasgow can mean as much as one-third absenteenism in some of the Clyde shipyards. The profit the S.F.A. makes from the New Year game is its own affair: it is providing a public service (and recreation *is* a public service, and a valuable one at that) and it deserves to be paid for it. It does *not* deserve to make a profit from the public disservice of lowering production and dislocating traffic during working hours, and I am with those people who say it should be stopped. There are plenty of Saturdays in the year.

What the historians of the future will make of all this is difficult to say. They may well find it astonishing that tens of thousands of people were prepared to leave their work, sacrifice their pay, and incur the displeasure of the foreman for the sake of a game of football. If it comes to that, I find it astonishing myself. Yet it happens. There is a clear case here for the politicians courting a little unpopularity and removing temptation from our way.

Police struggle to hold back a boisterous crowd thronging the streets of Edinburgh after a local team had won a Cup Final, one of the most exciting matches of the year. Extravagant and quite unwarranted forms of Scottish dress (on the opposite page) are all part of the fun when the fans turn out to support their teams on big occasions.

Early summer sees the many local Border common-riding festivals. Whole towns and villages take time off to participate.

Traditional fairs and festivals held in countless towns and villages provide fun annually for thousands of Scots. *Right:* An Orkney child in the showy and elaborate regalia of the ancient "Plowing Match" held on the sands of an island beach.

The Kate Kennedy procession is held in spring and provides fun for the students of St. Andrews University.

Braving the wild January weather, Shetlanders celebrate their ancient Up-Helly-Aa festival.

As the fishing season closes towards the end of September, striped petticoated fisherwomen dance in the streets of Musselburgh

*Left: a view across Loch Maree in Wester Ross to
Slioch, whose 3,217 ft. summit qualifies it as a Munro.
From the top of a great precipice on An Stac (below),
another Munro, a mountaineer looks out over Loch
Lurgainn.*

The Munro Hunters

FROM time to time people write to me and ask what a Munro is;
and since there has been some recent argument on the subject in
the Press it might be as well to settle the thing. A Munro is a Scottish
mountain of 3,000 feet or over which is not merely a shoulder of another
mountain but a peak in it own right. The distinction makes a difference.
There are 543 tops in Scotland which reach or exceed 3,000 feet, but
only 276 of them can claim a separate existence and the title of Munro.
For example, Ben Cruachan has seven tops over 3,000 feet high, but only
two of them qualify; and in the seven tops of Beinn Eighe there is only
one Munro. The Munroes are widely scattered. The most northerly is

Ben Hope in Sutherland; the most westerly Sgurr na Banachdich, in
Skye; the most easterly Mount Keen, on the Forfar-Aberdeenshire
border; and the most southerly and best-known, Ben Lomond.

They came by their name because an energetic baronet, Sir Hugh T.
Munro of Lindertis, climbed most of them and classified them all during
the latter part of the nineteenth century. Munro's Tables were published
in 1891, and since then have ranked with the Tables of Moses in the minds
of devout mountaineers, a fact which their wives have had reason to find
distressing.

The trouble has been that they have set a standard for the pot-hunter.
With the full list available on the shelf, some men collect mountains as
others collect stamps; and in extreme cases they are smitten with the desire
to climb the lot and leave the women to their knitting. It is an insidious
disease. I remember having a touch of it myself once. The other day I
came across my old copy of the Tables and saw again the pencil ticks in
the margin. I seem to have learned sense round about my thirtieth Munro.
Like most climbers I soon lost my taste for quantity as opposed to quality
and settled down to Nevis, Skye, the Glencoe peaks, and the little Cobbler
which is not a Munro at all and is worth five of most of them.

There are, nevertheless, several people who have climbed them all,
and at least one who tried to take in all the outlying tops as well. I met
him in pouring rain and dense mist on top of Beinn Chaluim (a bing if

ever there was one), anxiously wondering if he really was at the top. As I was anxiously wondering how quickly I could reach a hot bath I do not know what became of him. That was twenty years ago, so he should be on the last lap by now.

On the whole I disapprove of Munroes. A Munro-hunter in the party makes for restlessness—he always wants to do just one more before dusk or drag everyone up something which has nothing to commend it but its height—and frankly I do not think the big peaks and catalogues go well together. I do not care if Spidean a' Choire Leith is the 71st Munro and the 138th top. I just like that view you get down the north side of the ridge. Lists destroy the mystery.

The most notable Munro-hunter in my experience was a sturdy character who, though restless and fond of variety, did feel that he was in some way affronting the dignity of the mountains by trampling them all underfoot. When the great day came and he reached the last one, the 276th of his pilgrimage, he was going to stop fifty feet from the top. I have always wondered if he had the will-power to do it.

Not, of course, that the great day ever does come. Munro-hunters are haunted men. From time to time the 6-inch Ordnance Survey map is revised (a new revision is going on now) and as each edition comes from the press the effect of increasingly accurate instruments becomes apparent. Peaks hitherto believed to be Munroes have sunk below the 3,000-foot contour and others, remote and unclimbed others, have poked their heads above the surface. There is no end to it, no certainty. Munro-hunters, far from retiring to rest on their laurels, can only hope that old age has not overtaken them before the next revision is published.

In central Ross-shire a group of thirteen summits rises above the 3,000 ft. level. Nine of them are classed as Munroes, or separate mountains. Above, the shadowed peak of Sgurr Mor rises above the curving ridge called Meall nam Peithirean. On the right, climbers on the Isle of Skye in the Inner Hebrides, descend the Inaccessible Pinnacle of Sgurr-Dearg—the most difficult to reach of all hill summits.

The Unfair Fortnight

Clyde steamer tied up to a wet pier, embarking drenched holiday-makers from Glasgow during "Fair Fortnight". As a result of countless coincidences, it now seems that "Fair Fortnight" is traditionally one of the wettest of the year. Below: Fair crowds, well protected against the threatening weather, make the most of a wet day on the beach at Ayr.

WHENEVER autumn is upon us and we can look back over the holiday season, I am impressed all over again by the obstinacy of the citizens of Glasgow. Once again they have spent the Fair shivering in boarding-houses while the rain teemed down outside, lamenting as is their custom the vile habits of the weather in the month of July. It seems they will never learn.

It is close on seven hundred years now since William the Lion granted a charter " to God and St. Kentigern and Bishop Jocelyn and his successors " which gave, among other things, the right to hold a fair of eight days' duration in July, following the octaves of St. Peter and St. Paul; and seven hundred years is a long time during which to study the weather. In the beginning, admittedly, the Fair was mainly a market and it was the wretched incomers who had to drive their beasts to it in foul weather, but even so the Glaswegians must have noticed that it was far from being the dryest month of the year. Yet today the Fair Fortnight is still in July, and they will not have it otherwise.

July and August can, of course, be admirable months in the West; but the records show that one's chances are much better in May, June and September. The extreme case is the Isle of Skye. There was a period of four consecutive years in the 1930's when there was not a single dry day

A scene at Loch Morlich in the heart of the Highlands, where hundreds of young people from all over Scotland enjoy holidays all the year round. Below, private yachts taking part in one of the many summer yachting events off the West Coast of Scotland.

on Skye in August; yet by visiting the island in May, June and September I have had only one wet week in twelve. In a lesser degree this tendency is true of the rest of the western seaboard, where Glasgow for the most part spends its holidays.

Landladies dislike the Fair because it sets a quarter of the population of Scotland clamouring for beds at the same time. The railways dislike it for the same reason: Glasgow Central Station on Fair Saturday looks like a section of the terracing at a Cup Final. Shopkeepers at both ends dislike it because it dislocates their businesses. The Tourist Board dislikes it because it realises that the maximum prosperity of Scotland as a tourist country depends on a five-month season, not on a sudden burst in July.

For a time it seemed as if the Fair had weakened its grip, for during the war and for a few years after it works' holidays were staggered by order of the Government. One felt that an arrangement so clearly satisfactory to all concerned would persist, but public opinion was against it. The general feeling appeared to be that half the fun was lost when the magic date was altered, that hanging up stockings in November didn't bring Christmas Day next morning. Nearly all works' holidays in Scotland have reverted to dates in July, and a cancellation in a Rothesay boarding-house for this year's Fair drew 40 telegrams and 160 letters in two days.

Well, there it is. We are strange people. There is no doubt at all on which side wisdom lies, if by being wise we mean being practical. And yet one wonders about a feeling so ancient and so deep-rooted. I do not understand it, but I would be reluctant to tamper with it. Instincts are best left alone. And after all, it is their holiday

The popular Youth Hostel in Glen Doll, Angus.

Thousands of hostellers every year make use of Hailes House, Edinburgh.

The Youth Hostel Habit

ONCE upon a time, in September 1930, a friend of mine induced me to try a different kind of holiday. We bought rucksacks, and tickets to Fort Augustus, and in ten days we covered 150 miles beyond the Great Glen. In all that way we met only two people on the roads—a couple of tramps on Mam Ratagan.

The same route today swarms with youngsters either on bicycles or on foot, heading for the next youth hostel. When they get there, a nominal sum (I think it stands at half-a-crown at present) gets them a bed and blankets, and the use of the common-room and the pots and pans therein. In the morning they are off again, and once more there is a hostel at the day's end. Scotland is covered by a chain, close on 100 hostels for the young and impecunious, so placed that they are a day's march apart.

The Scottish Youth Hostel Association has over 40,000 members and is affiliated to similar organisations all over the world. The number of times its beds are used in a season is away up in the six-figure class, and the clientele is international.

All this has come about as a result of a meeting which was held while I was doing that first walk twenty-seven years ago. George Lansbury spoke in Glasgow, and in his speech he said something about " hostels for hikers ". The idea was picked up by a man called Dr. Alan Fothergill, who wrote to the *Scotsman* about it, saying this was a good thing that ought to be developed. Others followed, including an A. D. Smith who got right down to brass tacks by saying he would subscribe £5 if ninety-nine other people would do the same.

Fothergill gathered the enthusiasts together, and within six months of Lansbury's speech the Scottish Youth Hostel Association was launched with Lord Salvesen in the chair, and Fothergill as secretary. It has never looked back.

The Association never has as much money as it would like, but it has many voluntary helpers among its members, and over the years it has built up and extended its chain. The hostels vary greatly. Some are old mansion houses or castles, big places with over 100 beds in them. Others are converted cottages, holding only a few. Others again have been specially built by the Association in places where the demand is great and existing buildings inadequate. Each has a resident warden to supervise the running of the place. The word is " supervise ". The members themselves have to do the sweeping and the stoking and the chores before they leave in the morning.

The result is that, with no blankets, no tent, no pots and pans and little food to be carried, hiking becomes more of a pleasure and less of a weight-lifting contest. The Scottish countryside is wide open to anyone with the energy to walk ten miles or so in a day, with the occasional longer stretch. " Youth " is a relative word. Some members are in their seventies.

If I had to nominate the organisation which, in the past quarter century, had done the most good in Scotland for the least money spent, I should not hesitate.

Scottish youth hostellers on a typical hill walk through the incomparable Highland scenery.

An island Youth Hostel : Staffin on the Island of Skye.

A typical pair of holidaymaking hikers setting off after a night's stay in Glen Rosa on the Island of Arran.

This picture shows the arrival at Fingal's Cave of what was, so far as is known, the first canoe party ever to reach the Island of Staffa.

Shooting the gap in the Melrose Cauld, Lady Mears, Commodore of the Forth Canoe Club, and Mr. Ian Chisholm, Vice Commodore, manoeuvre their frail craft through "white water"

Above: a great deal of Highland energy is expended every year in the very old Celtic game of shinty. Quiet preoccupation, on the other hand, is the choice of many other Scots, who like nothing better than to spend the day with a rod and a favourite fly on a Highland river (right).

To the many older forms of Highland recreation has now been added pony-trekking. This new holiday idea has been enthusiastically taken up by young people from all over the United Kingdom.

Indoor rinks have made curling popular all the year round. Every year Scotland is the scene of international matches. Below: one of the many famous golf courses which annually attract so many spectators and players.

Highland dancing, unlike some other facets of Highland life, has undergone a vigorous revival. Dancers play a prominent part at Highland Games. The graceful Aboyne Dress (above, centre) is gradually replacing the kilts and bandsmen's tunics hitherto erroneously worn by some Scottish female dancers.

Putting the shot, as popular in the Highlands as elsewhere, attracts strong men from a wide area to the many games held annually in the country districts.

The Games (1952)

THE Aboyne decision to revert to traditional dress for girl dancers at the Games has met with two clearly defined receptions—unanimous praise from the Press and bitter opposition from the dancers themselves. The opposition does not, strangely enough, base its argument on the ground that no self-respecting female, however young, would be found dead in a garment designed by the Lord Lyon King of Arms, but instead claims that the kilt at present worn allows the subtle movements of the knees to be judged. This is nonsense. The fact is they love their horrid little kilts and bandsmen's tunics, and they adore their medals.

I am not overfond of the Lord Lyon's confection, however well rooted in tradition it may be. It is barely in the Hartnell, Worth, or Amies class. The tartan sash apart, it reminds one rather of Act One, Scene One of the the pantomime (enter chorus of village maidens) and is good taste so quiet as to be practically inaudible. However, if the Games cult is to claim a traditional basis, it would do well to follow traditions manufactured before the year 1900, and should welcome the chance of having the Lyon's official seal set upon the goings-on.

From this it may be inferred that I am not a great supporter of the Games. This is quite wrong. I know Highland games (some of them actually held in the Highlands) where the contestants are mainly local people; and if I can attend them I do, for they are grand fun. What I do not like is the travelling circus of professional sportsmen and dancers which tours the larger ones; and most of all I dislike the mothers of the little girls. The tots, one hopes, know no better. More culpable are the anxious mamas who deck out their offspring in mock-Highland dress and set them dancing with a couple of pounds of medals rattling on their chests.

For the dress—one might as well present girl singers in white tie and tails. For the dancing and the medals—what strange pride do the mothers draw from them? A psychologist on the look-out for a thesis might find rich stuff here.

The annual Highland Games held at Braemar, usually attended by members of the Royal Family, is one of the most spectacular and popular events of the Highland year.

Life in the Highlands

Hebrides (1947)

THE postman brought me a letter the other day that set me thinking. There was an idea in the letter; one of those ideas that seem so much better than the truth that I began to wonder if I were being a little fanciful about it. Yet it seemed to hold together. There was a simplicity about it that appealed to me and made me want to know more.

It came from a friend I had not seen for years, a parish priest in the Outer Isles, and it began with the usual tale of woe one hears about the Highlands . . . the falling population, the crofts lying in ruins, whole townships and series of townships going back into desert, areas where the young have gone to the cities and only the very old are left . . . the familiar story of the Celtic Twilight. So far he had nothing new to say. Nor was the second half of his story any less familiar. He pointed out that this general picture did not apply to the Outer Isles. There, he said, there was land hunger. There were not enough crofts to go round. And, in a land where there was no industry worth speaking about, a man had to have a croft to obtain even the most meagre prosperity.

Then came the idea. Land was going to waste on the mainland and the Inner Isles, and land was badly needed on the Outer Isles. Why, said the priest, not do a deal? Why not colonise the mainland with landless folk from across the Minch?

I suppose your reaction is very much what mine was. This is too easy. There must be a catch in it. General statements, however attractive, break down before facts and figures.

I wrote for facts and figures, and this was the reply:

" I can speak," said the priest, " for only one small corner of the Isles, but I think I can claim to know that corner well. I organised a public discussion in Benbecula, followed by a ceilidh, on the subject, ' Would it be more profitable to stay on the Highland crofts or reside in the cities?' It resulted in a vote of 96 per cent. in favour of crofts. I had similar results in South Uist and North Uist.

" I have also found that in North Uist, South Uist, Benbecula, and Barra, some six hundred young men and women under the age of twenty-five will never, due to local conditions, own a croft. There is no croft for them. The Crofters' Act, as you know, forbids squatters—and we don't want squatters. The eldest son usually gets the croft; and with the demise of the old parents and the son taking unto himself a wife, the rest of the family naturally turns its eyes to the cities. The home is no longer theirs. This method of the eldest son taking over the croft is mainly the key to many emigrations to the city. There is nothing else left for them.

" There is only one other way in which this difficulty is overcome. The majority of the young people prefer the land, and in some areas like North Uist and South Uist there is very little, a barely noticeable percentage, of emigration to the cities; but in its place is a far worse state of things—a hang on at home with the consent of the brother or sister owner of the croft. This creates innumerable bachelors. A rough calculation would produce a population thirty years hence made up of 50 per cent.

Uncertain communications and difficult transport are hazards of living in many parts of the Highlands. Here a bag of coal brought by steamer is hauled over a beach and up to a house on the island of Soay, off Skye.

One of the more important activities of a Highland crofter's year; sheep-shearing at the time of the summer wool clip.

Left: one of the most delightfully unspoiled of all Highland towns—Inveraray on the shore of Loch Fyne in Argyllshire.

A crofter's shieling on the Outer Hebridean island of Benbecula. Here the old Highland way of life is threatened with extinction by the establishment of a large-scale modern military project on South Uist.

The traditional Highland occupation of handloom weaving has grown into a profitable and flourishing "cottage industry".

bachelors. To avoid this certain state of affairs, as affecting at least the Hebrides, colonisation on the mainland of the young blood from the Isles is a generous act, in comparison with shifting them to Canada. . . ."

These figures impress me. Of course, six hundred landless folk are not going to solve the mainland's population problem even if all of them were willing to leave home. My friend's estimate, in fact, is that round about 250 of them would be willing to leave. But the mere suggestion of 250 youngsters in one corner of the Hebrides who would be willing to try their luck on the mainland is enough to set one's imagination working.

What could be in it? It is generally believed now that the future of the Highlands, if they have a future, lies not in isolated crofts with no amenities, but in new communities big enough to support the various social services, set up in specially favourable areas where fertile soil, forestry and hydro-electricity could combine to give a reasonable standard of living. At the lowest estimate, those four islands at the southern end of the Outer Isles could found one such community, and no doubt the other islands could supply the men and women for three or four more. It would at least give us a start, and prove once and for all if the community idea is practicable. The idea would spread once it had proved itself.

Have we so little enthusiasm left in Scotland, are we so bereft of ideals, that we can produce nothing to fire the imagination of a young man in Benbecula who has nothing before him but perpetual bachelordom or a flight to the city? He is good human material going to waste, and the mainland could be doing with him. Today all talk about the Highlands is either cold statistics about the present or romantic froth about the past.

Life in the Highlands and Islands is slower, steadier and more peaceful than in the bustling lowlands and industrialised areas of central Scotland. Here a crofter walks behind his team on the fertile machair of South Uist.

" They agreed that dishonesty was a terrible thing."

Highlanders and "The Sport"

SPORT is said to be an English invention (S P O R T spells sport in almost every European language) but I am tempted to believe that it was discovered independently in the Hebrides of Scotland. There is in the Isles an ancient fondness for the game played for its own sake which is so deeply rooted that it is part of the national character, though it is only fair to point out that most Englishmen would have difficulty in recognising it. It does not concern itself with trivial like cricket. For the most part it has to do with the Hebridean way of life.

There is, for example, the tale which is told of the Jura landowner who was troubled by the oldest professional sportsmen of all, the poachers. Having tried everything else and failed, he sought out the leading practitioner in the district, a gentleman who is still revered as the greatest West Coast poacher of the past three generations, and spoke to him as follows:

" Mr. So-and-So," he said, " do you like venison? "

Mr. So-and-So said that he did, but, man, it was long enough since he had tasted any.

" And do you like salmon? "

Ah, now, salmon was real tasty, but where would a man like him be getting salmon? There were rough fellows who lifted a fish from time to time; but that wasn't honest, now was it? It was a terrible thing dishonesty.

They agreed that dishonesty was a terrible thing.

" Well," said the landowner, " if ever you want a stag or a salmon, just you come over to my place and help yourself. Shoot what you like, and fish what you like. Your tastes do you credit, and I wouldn't see you living on mackerel."

The invitation was never accepted. At considerable inconvenience to himself the poacher transferred his attentions to a more distant estate where they played the game by the rules and a man might have some fun while he was earning his living.

That is typical Hebridean sportsmanship, and it extends to all manner of other fields, such as fleecing the Government, squeezing subsidies (pronounced sub*side*-ies) and the welcoming of wrecks. The greatest profit is not the true criterion: it is the game that counts.

I was arguing on these matters recently with my friend the inshore fisherman, and the evergreen subject of salvage came up. He spoke fondly of the season when he brought in two yachts, one dismasted and the other adrift, and was awarded £300 for the work of two afternoons.

Taking a salmon from the river, a tree from the forest, and a deer from the mountain, are three actions no Gael was ever ashamed of.
—Highland saying.

" But och, man, that's just *money*. Take wrecks, now. You'd be surprised how little you get off a wreck, even a good one. The folk go through her lifting and laying everything, carrying a thing a yard or two and then laying it down for something else. They canna make up their minds. And if the women are out, it's worse. Like a bargain sale, it is. Lifting and laying, lifting and laying, and before you know where you are the excisemen are on their way and it's a stampede. You probably get very little."

" Just so. That's why I should have thought that salvage, which is sure and legal——"

" Money. Just money. Give me a good wreck and a day's pilfering every time." A faraway look came into his eye. " A fair sea running, and the folk laughing, and everybody with five hundred cigarettes in his pocket. The ballast going overboard from your boat, and rum and wireless sets being stowed in its place. The excisemen just half an hour away, and coming up fast. Ah, yon's the life. There's seldom a profit in it, but it's the life all right. Salvage? You can keep it."

All of which goes to show that sport is not the prerogative of the English, nor does it necessarily involve striking a ball. In the Isles they make no bones about it. The word " poaching " is never used. Instead they always say " The Sport."

He that steals a cow from a poor widow, or a stirk from a cottar is a thief, but he that lifts a drove from a Sassenach is a gentleman-drover.
—Highland definition.

Sheep (1954)

" If poaching a salmon costs £50, then a sheep should be worth more."
Ben Wilson of Troloss.

MR. WILSON has a commanding presence, forthright views, and a voice which carries halfway across upper Clydesdale. He uses the voice for making unambiguous statements like the one quoted above.

I agree with him and with the Blackfaced Sheep Breeders' Association that circumstances have changed since the penalties for sheep-stealing were fixed and that new and stiffer penalties should be imposed. There is a fair analogy between salmon and sheep today. Both live in lonely country which is difficult to guard, both are at the mercy of any unscrupulous person with a motor-car or lorry, and both have increased so much in value that one beast pays the fine. Sheep-stealing has increased greatly in recent years and it is very difficult to cope with: not only is the flock widely scattered, but a sheep may not be missed for weeks.

Higher penalties would certainly do the trick. Alec Whamond, head water bailiff for Loch Lomond and the surrounding rivers, tells me that during the entire season following the increased fines for salmon poaching he had only nine prosecutions in his area. Before then he had sometimes had as many in a week.

£50 and/or six months for sheep as well as for salmon would go a long way towards stamping out something which is becoming a small modern industry.

Curiously enough, however, in this year of 1957 the Sassenachs in Parliament have still not changed the law for sheep or deer.

On the whole, Highland ways are going, but here and there tradition lingers on. In this picture a woman is using the age-old cas-chrom, or foot-plough near her old-style Highland homestead—which has, one notices, been wired for electricity.

Gaelic Up to Date

MANY years ago Norman Bruce wrote a radio revue in which the music was suddenly interrupted and a high-pitched Highland voice broke in.

"This week's Gaelic lesson," said the voice. "The Gaelic word for electreecity . . . iss electreecity. Listen at this time next week for *next* week's Gaelic lesson."

Now this was no more than the truth. The Gaelic language has acquired no new words in the past couple of hundred years or so as anyone who shops as I do in the Hebrides can testify. One stands at the counter listening to the incomprehensible noises issuing from one's neighbour, and every now and then from the spate of sound little islands of sense jut out. There is a flow of language, noble-sounding stuff with an air of antiquity about it, and then: " . . . two-and-sixpenny postal order. . . ."

One listens more carefully, thinking perhaps that the ear has been tricked; but no, it comes again: " . . . puncture repair outfit . . . wireless licence . . . and a pound pot of marmalade."

The Gaelic word for electricity is indeed electricity, hence the prize which has been put up by the Gaelic Society of London. It has been offered for the best set of twenty-five new Gaelic words submitted before the London mod is held in June, the idea being to find Gaelic equivalents for the many hundreds of new words which modern invention have brought to the English language.

As I do not have the Gaelic I shall be unable to appreciate the winning entries, but it will be interesting to see which English words have been chosen. Judging by conversations I have heard, what is most needed is a good sound translation of the words " Treble Chance ".

The Post-War Highlander

OUR guests, being very young, were easily amused. They spent most of their time fishing off the end of the jetty or snaring rabbits, which helped the pot and kept them out of mischief. One day they caught a baby rabbit, and were about to turn it loose when it occurred to them that young Patrick, aged two, might like to see it first. They brought it into the house, and held it in front of him, stroking it and saying, " Pretty bunny, pretty bunny," or words to that effect.

But Patrick had been born and brought up in the hard post-war school, and had no time for such frivolities. His eye lit up. A look of pleasure crossed his face, and gave way to one more purposeful. He pointed, and breathed one word with great intensity.

" Meat! " said Patrick.

Ferry (1953)

ONE event which received little attention from the Press was the recent opening of the Luing ferry, which links the island with the mainland near Oban across the three-quarter-mile Cuan Sound, and is the first free ferry in Scotland.

The Press, living on a somewhat bigger island than some of us do in the West, had other fish to fry that day; but it was an event which sounded sweet in Hebridean ears. Living as I once did on a seashore where it cost me 15s. return to buy my groceries at a shop less than a mile away, I share with the native islanders and those who live by the sea-lochs of the mainland the opinion that all ferries would be free if there were any justice in the world. After all, the mainlander has his road, and either the Government or the local authority pays for it. If there is a gap in the road and a bridge is built across it, they still pay for it. But for some reason which eludes me the cost bounces back on the individual if the gap is such that a boat must ply across it.

Tourists are not amused, and in some cases local people suffer hardship. They pay their rates and their taxes, and they have as much right to a free sea-way as anyone else has to a trunk road. I hope that when the Ministry of Transport granted £18,000 to the Luing ferry it recognised this fact, and that the boat now plying across Cuan Sound with cars, lorries, cattle and passengers aboard is going to be the first of many.

The scene on the jetty at Port Askaig, Isle of Islay, on the day when the eagerly-awaited mail steamer calls to unload its cargo at the pier's end.

Tailpiece

FOR no reason at all I shall now tell my favourite story of the late Captain Duncan Robertson, for many years skipper of the *Lochmor* on the Lochboisdale run. It is a newspaper story, and I once told it at lunch to the appropriate editor. Some day I hope to have the pleasure of telling it to the appropriate press lord, for the good of his soul. For our present purpose we shall call the newspaper (one of the larger and more breathless dailies) the *Clarion*.

Captain Robertson was a small, round, red-faced man with gooseberry eyes and a penetrating high-pitched voice which was famous throughout the Hebrides. He feared neither man nor David MacBrayne, his wit was deadly, and he was greatly loved. One day a reporter from this newspaper which we are calling the *Clarion* crossed the Minch, heard some of the Captain's *beaux mots*, and on his return published them. On the following year he boarded the *Lochmor* again, and on the crossing noticed that the Captain was avoiding him in a most ostentatious way. At last, however, they met head on. The Captain spat over the rail and regarded him sourly.

"Hah!" said he. "And you would pe the young chournalist that crossed with us last year. Hm. And you wass writing stories about me. Hm. I wass fery offended py these stories, fery offended inteed. I tell you, I wass nearly writing to your tirectors about them. But, och, the *Clarion* . . ." A vast empurpled scorn grew on his face. ". . . the *Clarion*. It's like the cod. It'll take anything."

A typical Highland scene, showing the blue water of Loch Duich and the spectacular hills of Kintail.

Part of the motley cargo of livestock and vital supplies of all kinds carried by a steamer serving remote and otherwise inaccessible island communities.

Seaweed gathering on South Uist for the new island industry which has provided a profitable sideline for the crofters.

Highland cattle cooling themselves in the water of a shallow inlet in South Uist. A typical island crofthouse stands in the background.

Edge of the World (1948)

TALKING of planning and population problems reminds me that I had a letter the other day from Alexander Cullen, who is planning officer for the county of Inverness. His domains are wide and scattered, and his troubles are not far to seek. He sent me a paper he had written about one of these troubles, the island of South Uist, in the Outer Hebrides.

Cullen believes that South Uist has a future, and he spends much of his paper in explaining how this future could be realised; but for most people on the mainland, and especially in the cities, I think I had better pass on what he had to say about the living conditions on certain parts of the island just now. If you live within sound of the tram-cars and within sight of the shops, try to realise that only ninety minutes away by air, in modern Scotland, these conditions exist.

The main road down the spine of the island, built during the war to serve Benbecula airport, bypasses nearly all the townships, which lie miles off on the Atlantic seaboard. There are today isolated communities where all foodstuffs, fuel, stores, and building materials have to be carried on men's backs. Work out the weight of food and fuel used in your house in one day, and you will see what that means.

The neighbouring island of Eriskay has no road and no pier. The population is 500. The first motor vehicle ever seen on the island was brought there temporarily by a firm of contractors last year. The people there barely glance upwards at an aeroplane, but the lorry created a sensation.

Most of the townships have no tap-water, and have to rely on wells and pools, many of them verging on the undrinkable, and most of them liable to run dry in drought. Last summer some crofters lost three-quarters of their breeding stock through lack of water.

Nearly half of South Uist's thousand houses are thatched. Most of them consist of only two rooms. Here is Cullen's survey of a specimen which he says is typical:

" The entrance is by a doorway only five feet high, giving access to a single apartment, twenty-three feet long by twelve wide, which is divided by a cloth curtain into two compartments. The walls are built of stone to a thickness of three feet six inches. The floor is of earth, and internally the walls are damp and unlined. A solitary window, two feet wide, lights the living-room portion of the house, the curtained-off sleeping area having no natural light at all, and only a small ventilation opening at ceiling-level. Water is drawn from a near-by well of doubtful quality, and a primitive dry-earth closet is situated close to the building. In this house, five adults presently live."

It is not surprising when he adds that men greatly outnumber the women on the island. The women leave: a crofter only has to sleep in his house, but his wife has to live and work in it.

It is into this place that hydro-electricity is shortly to come, and the new seaweed industry has already arrived. The county is trying to provide new roads and new houses, battling against shortages and the fact that a four-roomed house costs at least £800 more to build out there than it does on the mainland, a factor which the Government housing grants do not cover. The regional water scheme is still a pious hope, but it should come to something some day. When it does it will make a tourist trade possible and allow expansion to take place in the seaweed and weaving industries.

Given these things, South Uist could thrive. Meantime it represents a state of affairs which the Scottish city-dweller has been quite incapable of imagining for at least the past two centuries. Over four thousand people live there.

A Song in South Uist

ON the other hand, there is one way in which the Gael keeps very much abreast of the times. I remember once being out in South Uist with Frank Collinson, getting together a " Country Magazine " broadcast, and while we were talking over the script in my room at Lochboisdale Hotel we heard a lad singing as he polished a car outside.

He had a good voice, and Frank's concern was the music in the programme, so in a few minutes the three of us were in the public bar where, as all the world knows, matters of business in Lochboisdale are invariably settled. Frank asked the lad to sing, which he did, first telling us that the song's title was something unpronounceable meaning " Farewell to Glasgow ".

It was an apt title, for the song was like sad sea waves breaking on the beach. It would, I thought, be about emigrants torn from their homeland embarking for far places. The bar in general, however, thought otherwise. It was a very long song, and as verse succeeded verse the trawlermen who were fortifying themselves there first chuckled and then roared with laughter. When it ended with loud applause and many drams offered, I asked what it had all been about. The only recurring word I had been able to catch had been something which sounded like " airship ".

" Och," said the lad, " it was about Donald during the war there. He missed the boat at the end of his leave and had to take the aeroplane. And there was trouble about his travel warrant."

That was the first time I realised that folk music in the Outer Isles is still a living thing, not necessarily a tradition heard from grandfather who had it from his grandfather, but something which is constantly recreating itself. On that island alone many scores of genuine modern folk-songs are composed each year. In fact, our friend who polished the car turns up at the bar with a new one most Saturday nights.

Unlike the house in the story told on this page, electricitiy has arrived at this crofter's home and now, by courtesy of the North of Scotland Hydro-Electric Board, he is installing equipment which will make his wife's daily darg immeasurably easier. Right: Highland crofters gather at a special electricity exhibition at the Royal Highland Show in Inverness.

The Pamphlet (1947)

AFTER handing in my mail the other day, the postman dived into his pocket and produced a little pamphlet.

" I nearly forgot this," he said. " It's important. I've to deliver one at every house."

It was headed THE FUEL CRISIS AND YOU, and started off: " How can you save that vital quarter of your gas and electricity? "

This interested me. I read on. " The first steps," said the pamphlet, " are (1) Get to know your meters and read them regularly. (2) Find out your consumption last summer and arrive at your target figure. (3) Know how much fuel each gas and electrical appliance uses."

It was most interesting. I read it all down to the bit where they asked me to fill in my last summer's consumption and post it to my gas or electricity showroom.

" Have you filled in your form yet? " I asked the postman.

" No," said he.

" How many of these have you delivered so far? "

" Eighteen. I've twenty more to do."

" Everybody gets one? "

" Everybody."

" Well, well! " said I.

" Well, well! " said the postman.

It would be interesting to know who sends these things out. I live on the Isle of Jura. There is no gas or electricity on the island, never has been,

and probably never will be. I didn't mind them sending me that copy of the Highway Code—after all, one car passes my door every second day, and the state of the road does permit it to travel at fully fifteen miles an hour—but I can't help feeling that the time has now come for those chaps in London to be taught a little geography.

The belt plate produced for Sir John Sinclair's Fencibles in 1794.

Scotland's Statistical Account

by that time to bother about the future. It was not until the late 1940s that it was revived, with the result that the Third Account is being written at this moment.

It seems to me, looking back over these Accounts, that we have been extraordinarily lucky in their timing. The first appeared immediately before the Industrial Revolution and caught the old Scotland just in time. It gives us a complete and exact picture of a country which has vanished. The second appeared as the effects of the Industrial Revolution were beginning to be felt, so that we can see the changes it brought with it. The third, coming at the beginning of the atomic age, should with any luck be as strange to our descendants as the first is to us.

It astonished me that this project, getting on for two hundred years old now, should be so little known to the average Scot; or that so few people should take the trouble to walk into a public library and turn up their own parish. All sorts of things are there. For example, when I say elsewhere in this book that on the Isle of Islay whisky in the eighteenth century was a thing one made at the bottom of one's garden, I know I am telling the truth, because the minister all those years ago wrote it all down. He said there was hardly a cottage without its still. He also said: " The air is salubrious and the women of the parish live to a great age; but the men, thanks to their addiction to ardent spirits, die young ".

In the Second Account there is no mention of distilling. In those fifty years the excisemen had done their work and stamped it out.

Once, when I was week-ending regularly in Glencoe, I looked it up, and found this: " Crimes of an enormous nature are hardly known here. No instance of suicide or murder has occurred for twenty-five years past. . . . No inhabitants of these extensive parishes has been executed or banished for twenty-five years. One or two persons, guilty of irregularities, voluntarily banished themselves."

And so on, and so on. Both the early accounts are goldmines, and one could quarry indefinitely.

The Third Account, of which the first volume or two have been published, is a much more ambitious affair than its predecessors, as is natural in a society which has grown increasingly complex. In the volume on Ayrshire, for instance, many hundreds of investigators were employed, and the findings include all sorts of curious but vivid information ranging from recipes to the amount gambled nightly by the average dog-track devotee. I can see the writers of the future rubbing their hands. It is rich stuff.

Sir John Sinclair started something more far-reaching than he knew. He gave us not only a picture of Scotland in his own day, but gave us the habit of looking at ourselves in the mirror every half-century or so. Historians are going to bless him for as long as we have a history to write.

THE Statistical Account may seem to be an oddly brilliant idea, something so far out of the ordinary that one cannot imagine how a man could stumble on it; but though it is a brilliant idea there was nothing very odd about it at the time when it was conceived. Building for the future was a habit then. Men planted beech avenues before their mansions and oaks in their parks, knowing they would not be worth looking at in their own lifetime. They built country houses which have survived everything except death duties. They saw nothing in the least extraordinary in planning for their grandchildren and great-grandchildren.

Sir John Sinclair of Ulbster merely extended this habit, and planned a book for readers not yet born.

The idea had a grand simplicity. He would bully or cajole every minister in Scotland to write an account of his parish, describing its fauna, flora, population, industries and anything else about it that might be of interest; and then he would issue these as a series of volumes which would give a complete picture of Scotland. Like a photographer with a modern high-speed camera, he would fix an entire country in mid-career, make permanent a moment of time.

He did it, too. The reports rolled in, and the first volume was issued in 1791. Over the next few years the other volumes followed. This was the First Statistical Account.

Fifty years later it was felt the time had come to repeat Sir John's work, and the Second Statistical Account was prepared.

Thereafter, the idea languished. There should have been a new Account in the 1870s, but everyone was too much concerned with the present

Sir John Sinclair of Ulbster was undoubtedly one of the most energetic and enterprising Scotsmen who has ever lived. In a life packed with achievement he found time to initiate the now famous Statistical Account of Scotland, and to raise the Rothesay and Caithness Fencibles, whose uniform he designed.

The above portrait by Raeburn, on loan to the National Galleries of Scotland, Edinburgh, is reproduced here by permission of the owner, The Viscount Thurso, and through the courtesy of The Medici Society Ltd., London.

6

47

Peat

IN the early summer the Highlander, laughing heartily at the price of coal, departs with his family to the bog and begins work on the long trench which his father and his father's father dug there. It is usually so wide that it is no longer a trench. Facing one wall, he sees a little cliff of peat about three feet high stretching away on either hand for several hundred feet. He starts at one end of this wall, using a spade with a lug on one side of the blade which allows him to make a right-angled cut; and for a week or two he works gently along, slicing out the peats and laying them behind him flat on the ground. He has to lay them flat because they are so wet and soft that they would break if they were left unsupported.

By the time he has dug down three spits, the whole length of the face has three orderly rows of peats lying beside it. The sun has been drying them out, so the children cock them up in little stooks so that the wind can get at them better. Later in the season they are brought home and built into a stack, and that is that until next year.

That is the process which has been carried out in one form or another in the Scottish Highlands for at least a thousand years and has given rise to those romantic pictures of the thatched cottage in the glen with the blue peat reek rising from the chimney and the woman smooring the fire at nightfall. It is a pleasant picture and I would be the last to deny that of all the blessings known to man there are few so comforting or so fragrant as a good peat fire.

The Flicks (1947)

A study in expressions as a young Highland audience, perhaps thirty or fifty miles from the nearest proper cinema, watches a cartoon.

It has been suggested that the English might be allowed to colonise the Colonies. It has even been suggested that the English might be allowed to colonise England. But in either case the insuperable difficulty arises—one is not within three miles of a cinema.

G. K. CHESTERTON.

OR, to bring the test a little nearer home, take the parish of Strontian, in Ardgour. The planners talk of forestry and electricity and the tourist trade, they produce graphs and population-pyramids; but Dr. Fraser Darling has said that the people of Strontian are far more interested in the arrival of a cinema than they are in anything the Hydro-Electricity Board may do for them. Tap-water and the end of paraffin lamps are one thing, but what Ardgour wants most is Hedy Lamar. And so says most of rural Scotland.

The audience is scattered, and so the Highlands have never attracted the commercial cinema to any great extent. Even travelling cinemas have seldom flourished, the principal difficulty being the cost of the equipment, the initial outlay. However, before the war one or two people in Scotland were beginning to wonder if there might not be a way round this difficulty. One of them was an Islayman called A. McNeil Weir, a young man with plenty of enthusiasm and one of the most mobile tongues west of the Scottish mainland. His theory was simple. All you had to do was find someone likely to buy your projectors for you, and then start talking. With the capital costs assured, a chain of travelling cinemas would pay its own way. The only problem was who to talk to.

After the war he found himself in the Scottish Agricultural Organisation Society, still thumping his big drum of Flicks for the Highlands. The Organisation was sympathetic, and the first people to listen were the Carnegie Trustees. He got two projectors, and was about to start when St. Andrew's House stepped in. It seemed the M.O.I. had travelling projectors. True, the Scottish branch of the Ministry was soon to be re-christened the Scottish Information Office, and would continue to show Government documentaries in remote parts of the country. Equally true, pep-films for farmers brought Hedy Lamar no nearer. But perhaps some compromise might. . . .

In the end it resolved itself into this. A large number of bodies, both public and private, had a direct interest in the business. The Highlanders wanted entertainment films. The Scottish Information Office wanted documentaries, and so did the Departments of Health and Agriculture: they had ideas, new techniques, they wanted to put over. And the Education Department knew that so far as school films were concerned, Scotland was one of the most backward countries in western Europe. Young Farmers' Club and the W.R.I. wanted specialist films. The Forestry Commission wanted entertainment for their workers . . . and the S.I.O. had all those little vans with the projectors and generators inside.

It took a long time. The interdepartmental juggling was going strong a year ago when I first heard of the scheme. Nevertheless, it worked out in the end. The Highlands and Islands Film Guild (Hon. Secretary, A. McNeil Weir) was born, and on 21st April this year (1947), it gave its first show. It took place in a village hall in Hillswick, Shetland.

The methods used in Shetland are a fair sample of what is in store for the Highlands and the rest of the islands; and they are not without interest. The unit—which is simply a generator, a projector, and a few cans of film stowed away in a tiny 5-cwt. van—is giving forty shows a month. Twenty of them are to schools in the afternoons, and the other twenty to the public at large in the evenings. In April, the children who learned their lessons by film early in the day went along to the hall, or barn, or hayloft in the evening and saw *Mr. Deeds*. Many of them had never heard a talkie before. Five days a week the van moved on to another village. And the plan for the future is that if anyone else wants a show of a special kind—a club, or the W.R.I., or (and this has already been done at the Loch Sloy dam) if the workers on some isolated site are finding their spare time heavy on their hands—if, as I say, any of these or similar organisations want anything shown from documentaries to straight entertainment, then the projector and operator will be made available, They are there to be used.

The scheme has started well. The immediate aim of one unit per crofter country is already well on the way to being satisfied. Shetland began in April. By the end of this month there should be a unit in Caithness. Next month, Inverness and Argyll will have their units; and by August the Outer Isles will have theirs. That is a very fair start.

It may be a little difficult for the city-dweller to realise how much these shows are going to mean in the Highlands. They are going to mean much more than one night's entertainment a month in a string of out-of-the-way villages. To my mind, their chief advantage is that they are going to form a nucleus round which other things can be built. Unknown to most people who live in towns or cities, there are in the remoter parts of our country little organisations called community clubs. One that I happen to know started in a hayloft in the middle of a wild stretch of moorland measuring ten miles by six, population about sixty. Until the club was formed, these sixty people had practically no form of entertainment whatever, no sort of excuse to make the five- or six-mile trip by bicycle which had to be made before they could get together. There might be a dance once or twice a year, but that was all until an enterprising land-owner started the club and gave these people something to look forward to once a fortnight. It was a simple enough affair, but it caught on. Every second Saturday, people began to trickle in from the outlying crofts for a chat, and a dance, with perhaps a lecture or a piping class thrown in. The club gave some sort of centre to their lives. It became so popular that everyone who was well enough, or young enough, began to attend it.

There are scores of these clubs in Scotland, operating under difficulties similar to the one I have mentioned. Their weakness is the one common to all such enterprises. With little ready-made material to hand, they depend almost entirely on the personality of the man or woman who is running them. The man with a flair is successful. The man without it is not. But when you fit films into that background, the picture is very different. The film, and not the organiser, carries the weight of the job. The magnet is there, ready made. Round it, in time, can be grouped the other activities which make leisure worth living in these very remote places. Once a month there is a reason why a community should be a community, and not just a scatter of crofts.

The Highlands and Islands Film Guild is a very good idea, and it has possibilities. It may be that it will not always be necessary to subsidise each new unit. Some districts, of course, must always operate at a loss ; but others are more populous and may show a profit. I suspect, for example, that the profit in Skye might cover the loss in Tiree, and that the Outer Isles should be able to produce profitable audiences. We shall see. Five circuits are working or about to work; but I have an idea that this is only the beginning.

Note.—It was. In the ten years which have passed since this paragraph was written, the travelling cinema has become an accepted part of life in the Highlands. Weekly shows are now operating in most districts.

Men of the Hills

OUR native blackface sheep, bred on the hill and picking a bite here and there in winter as best it can, has a flavour that none of your puffed-up creatures from the Sussex Downs can ever equal. Properly roasted it is one of the great dishes of Scotland.

My friend Geordie, who is a shepherd to trade and a wise man, declares that if sheep had the sense not to overdo the clover and the frosted turnips, then his job would be a lot easier than it is. They are heir to forty-eight different diseases, mostly brought on by stupidity; but at least, he says, they are regular in their habits. If they were not, our shepherds would be hard put to it.

The Scottish sheep, either in the Highlands or in the Lowlands, lives rough and high. Bad weather can snow it under, and there have been years when losses have been heavy. If it were not for this regularity of habit, the losses would be worse than they are.

Geordie explains it like this. If one goes into a restaurant where there are regular customers, one knows perfectly well that at, say, 12.30, the big man with the red face will be at such-and-such a table. It is the same with sheep. When a sheep is caught without warning and is snowed under, the shepherd must know where to dig. He does know, because the whole bare hillside is like the restaurant: he can say with complete certainty that at, say, 12.30, the cross-bred ewe with the limp was grazing by the big rock at the whins. The storm broke then, so there she will be.

The man who can do that 500 times over, once for every sheep he has, is a good shepherd. Geordie says there is no saying what a sheep will do, sheep being daft enough for anything; but when it has done a thing once it will go on doing it for life.

Many Scots, living in lonely places, are engaged in various stages of production for the country's wool industry.

These well-designed new buildings in Glasgow won the Saltire Award for the best flats built in Scotland during the year 1951. Below: Charles Rennie Mackintosh's " Willow Tearooms", Glasgow. It comes as a surprise to learn that this design dates from 1904. Mackintosh was a man who saw far ahead of his day and generation.

Design in Scotland

Do we have good taste?

DOES the average Scotsman have good taste? The Scottish Committee of the Council of Industrial Design says no, and in saying it has brought a good deal of criticism down about its ears. It has been suggested in the correspondence columns of the press that statements of this sort (". . . a lamentable appreciation of the difference between a good-looking object and a bad-looking one " were the words used) are a poor advertisement for Scottish goods, the implication being that so long as our best firms employ good designers it behoves the Council to hold its tongue.

The what-will-the-neighbours-think argument has never appealed to me very much. Of course we have good designers (in recent years, to name only one case, a Scottish textile firm designed a plain woollen scarf that has sold in its thousands right round the world) but the question surely is twofold. First, have we enough of them? And second, do we, the customers, know enough about it to encourage them by buying their wares?

I would answer no to both questions. There are too many bad designers at large, and we accept too much of their work. The commonest examples of all are the houses we live in. There is one very odd fact about the houses built between the two wars which is not generally known but which is only too true; and it is that in a vast number of cases no architect was employed in the building of them. Local authorities, fully aware of the need for employing a surveyor to level their sites and plan their roads, saw no reason to employ an expert to design their houses. They left it to the builder, with results which will be with our grandchildren if the wretched things stand up long enough. And we didn't stop them.

We let them put panelled doors in our houses, each with sixteen extra edges to be dusted daily. We let them install kitchen sinks below waist-level. We bought clocks with square faces and put them on our mantelpieces. We knocked tiled bathroom walls to pieces in trying to fix towel rails and fittings which should have been there in the first place. These things have nothing to do with design? Of course they have. They *are* design.

Design means planning something that will do its job efficiently, and look good while it is doing it. And nine times out of ten if it is efficient it will look good in any case. Since we have started on modern houses, let's fit that definition to Scottish houses in the past. Let us take the most primitive example of all, the Hebridean black house.

With modern materials we can build homes today which are more efficient and comfortable than the black house, and therefore it is right that they should be dying out. But when they were first designed, they were the complete answer to crude materials and Atlantic gales. They had double walls with the stones sloping towards the centre and earth packed between, to trap the damp blown into them by the wind. The roof, which would have been blown off if it had been overhung, ended between the walls, so that the rain ran down between them and kept the earth damp and windproof. The house had rounded ends, streamlined against the wind. Looking at them casually now, we say they " fit " the landscape. What we actually mean is that the landscape has made them—they are as they are because the Hebrides supplied stone, straw thatch, and wind, and some genius came along and adapted a house to those three things.

And so it is with all traditional design—Swiss chalets with enormous eaves to carry the snow away, Dutch roofs steeply pitched to cope with heavy rainfall, Suffolk cottages overhanging storey by storey lest the rain soak into their plaster walls. The black house takes its place in a great company of houses which are comely because they are efficient.

And now? Well . . . have you seen the Council houses at Kyle of Lochalsh, or that little group of horrors beyond the old bridge at Killin?

Our telephone receivers have improved, but have our lamp-posts kept pace? Can we conscientiously say we don't buy things just because they look different, like the square teapot I saw the other day? Do we ask ourselves why most of the pans made since the war have handles which become too hot to hold, and table-lamps are so tall they can hardly keep their balance? Shortage of materials has nothing to do with any of these things. They are just examples of bad design.

It has been suggested that we should hold an Exhibition of Good Design in Everyday Things. This seems to me an altogether excellent idea, for the more we are educated in these matters the more will manufacturers be encouraged to design well. But more is needed. If Scotland is once more to build up an export market for herself, it is time that many more manufacturers paid their designers sufficiently well to attract the best men. As in our pre-war housing, far too little of the work has been in the hands of the expert, and it has not been so in other countries. Czech glass, Viennese embroidery, Brussels lace, Copenhagen china can all be recognised on sight. It is time we had another Paisley Pattern, not in one industry, but in hundreds.

Since the last war there has been a revival of interest in handcrafts of all kinds. Right: a Shetland crofter makes a traditional " kishie," which will be eagerly snapped up by visiting tourists. Below: the Scottish Craft Centre in Edinburgh is one of many organisations presenting Scottish crafts to an appreciative international public.

Along with the interest in Arts and Crafts has arisen a fashion in Scottish fabrics, ornamented with handmade jewellery in Celtic style. The latter makes use of semi-precious stones found in the Highlands and Islands, and of pearls from Scottish rivers—particularly the Tay.

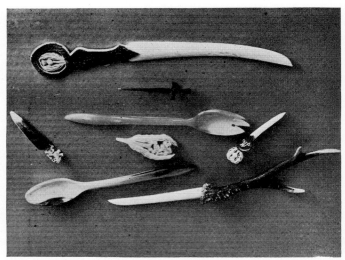

The intricate work of a horn carver, making use of raw material supplied from the moors and glens of the Highlands.

Souvenirs and the Tourist

IF you have had any experience of very young children, you will know that when they go to a party they must all win a prize. However inept at musical chairs young Johnnie may be, or however large the gaps in his rendering of " Wee Willie Winkie " he must get something. If he doesn't, he howls. It seemed to me that the same technique was used by the Scottish Committee of the Council of Industrial Design when it held its souvenir competition. There were sixty-seven prizes.

The Council, of course, has a difficult job to do. In a land where tartan tea-cosies and celluloid dolls in kilts pass as the highest examples of the souvenir manufacturer's art, any piece of work with pretensions to quality or originality deserves a pat on the back and a little encouragement. That, however, is only half the Council's problem. The other half is the public, the great mass of people who like to round off a holiday by taking something home, either for themselves or their friends; and the public at the moment is well content with tea-cosies. Until, by steady salesmanship, it is brought round to liking something better, the original artist might as well pack up and go home, for artists must eat, and in this particular class of work they have no market.

Already some prestige attaches to the Council's awards. Some people are prepared to back its judgment by buying goods of which it approves. It seems to me dangerous that it should give " encouragement " prizes for articles which are of anything less than the highest standard. It did just that with at least half of the sixty-seven prizewinners.

I would not like to give the wrong impression. Some of the entries were pretty terrible, but by and large the collection was a much better one than any previously gathered in Scotland, and all the prizewinners had something better than the usual run-of-the-mill to offer. The competition was a good idea, and the results were encouraging. They also showed, however, that we have a long way to go.

Those who had gone farthest had done so in an unexpected direction, and that interested me. Some of the competitors had tried very hard to be original (one of them had thought up a small whisky barrel which played " Auld Lang Syne ", an invention worthy of Dr. Strabismus himself), but the best of the bunch had concentrated on doing a simple job very well rather than racking their brains for something new. The best thing in the whole show, to my mind, was an ashtray designed by Kathleen F. Horsman. All souvenir-hunters want ashtrays, so it was a good thing to make. It had a beautifully drawn grouse on it, and so it was a good thing to have. It was just an ashtray, well done. The entry the judges liked best was a set of table-mats by G. W. Lennox Paterson. They were hand-printed with a design based on ancient Scottish stone carvings, and they were very good indeed. But there was nothing very original about the basic idea. They were just table-mats. And all through the exhibition I found the same thing: that everywhere the artist working

Edinburgh Crystal, produced in accordance with traditions of long standing, is making a name for itself all over the world.

A dirk, leatherwork, jewellery and a handwoven pure silk tartan scarf—craft work typical of what appeals to so many overseas visitors as presents to take home with them.

on a simple idea was producing a better article than the people who, in their efforts to avoid tartan, were saddling themselves with bizarre materials and unlikely shapes.

There was one exception to this, and it was worth noting. They were the products of our oldest crafts, the unselfconscious things turned out by people who made them that way because they had always been made that way. These, and the two articles I have already mentioned, were the only things I would care to match against the contents of any souvenir shop in Sweden; and they were all moderately expensive. No one, so far as I could see, had solved the problem of being cheap and amusing, as the Swiss woodcarvers have.

It took the Danes twenty-five years to build up their souvenir trade into the flawless thing it is now, so perhaps one cannot expect Scotland to catch up overnight. The Council is to be congratulated on doing as much as it already has done towards founding what could well be a prosperous industry.

A model shows off an example of the Border knitwear which now brings hundreds of thousands of dollars to a group of small towns in the South of Scotland. Below: a potter and his wheel quickly collect a crowd at a demonstration in an Edinburgh shop window.

From top to bottom—aluminium stew pans made in Scotland for home and export markets; a stoneware pottery grill pan produced by an old-established Edinburgh firm; a compact hot water boiler made of cast iron and steel: all attractive and efficient products of the industrial life of Scotland.

Furniture Fashions

IT was heartening to see, tucked away in a forest of ill-treated timber at a Furniture Exhibition in London, a number of Scottish exhibits of the very highest quality.

Since the war, the Scottish Furniture Manufacturers' Association has been trying hard to give the country a name for quality. By granting travelling scholarships and in other ways it has encouraged lads and lasses of parts to take up furniture designing as a career; and in collaboration with the Council of Industrial Design it has provided a pool of established designers on which its members can call. It has been a wise policy. It is as cheap to design well as badly, and there is always somebody on the lookout for something away from the usual run. Competition in this department is weak, most firms taking the line that the lowest common denominator in public taste is the safest one to choose. Lately we have been designing the best furniture in Britain, and it now seems that England is beginning to notice it. It would have been exceptionally short-sighted if it had failed to do so. The rest of the exhibition was deplorable.

Less than a year ago the managers of furniture shops were telling me that modern furniture wouldn't sell. Most people, they said, were conservative in their tastes, and those who weren't preferred this little line here—this little line being the type of bad 1920 to which the horrible word " modernistic " is usually applied. The idea appeared to be that almost anything would sell provided the design was sufficiently revolting. Why? Because the public liked it.

There was a fair amount of truth in this, and there still is. If, however, you take a quiet walk around the showrooms today you will notice that the best of the post-war stuff is beginning to make headway. The few firms which had the courage to specialise in it from the start are selling more; and the others, cautiously but increasingly, are beginning to experiment.

I think that soon a great deal more of the new furniture will be sold. I went down recently to see the show house in the new town of East Kilbride, and I heard what the people were saying as they passed through.

The house had been furnished by the Scottish Committee of the Council of Industrial Design, and they had made a good job of it. They had made a sensible job of it, too. Nothing in it carried tax—everything was utility—and nothing in it was hard to get. You could walk into half-a-dozen Glasgow shops and buy the lot if you wanted to. A printed list told you where, and how much. The furniture itself was excellent, and the wilder examples of modern design had been avoided. It was not the kind of thing most people buy, but it looked a wonderful house to live in. More than a thousand assorted housewives trooped through it in one day, and nearly all of them liked it. Most of them made a beeline for the price-list on the way out. So, I hear, did two city furniture dealers of the staider sort. They were looking thoughtful.

All in all it was a success which proved at least two things. First, East Kilbride (the first completely new town to be built in Scotland this century) is going to be a pleasanter place to live in than any other " council house " scheme I have seen. The houses, as all houses are these days, are tiny: they cost no more and use no more materials than any others. But somewhere an architect has been found with the ability to take these limitations and build a home out of them instead of a rabbit hutch. They are cheerful little houses. Second, the new furniture cannot be seen to advantage in a big showroom. It is utility furniture designed for the utility house, and it came as a shock to most of the people I spoke to that day to see what it could do for such a house.

For the sake of making it appear lived-in, the Council had included such things as a bicycle, children's toys, musical instruments, and other things which cannot fairly be reckoned as furniture. Making allowance for these on the price-list, I calculated that this five-room-and-kitchen house had been furnished down to the last detail for a fraction over £700. This included carpets on the floors, pictures on the walls, utensils in the kitchen, everything. That is not exactly small change, but the place looked downright luxurious. How many places do, these days, after £700 has been spent on them? How many places do with nothing to work on but utility? For that matter, how many places *are* fully furnished on less than £140 a room?

Scottish knitwear, much of which emanates from a highly enterprising group of Border towns, is enthusiastically sought after by women of many nations. A steadily increasing demand in recent years has sent Scotland's woollen products to selected stores all over the world.

The outsider romps home

I MET two happy people the other day. They made furniture, and they had just seen an outsider romp home at long odds.

I think I mentioned some months ago that furniture manufacturers in Scotland were having the imagination to spend money on design, both in the form of commissioning first-rate men to do work for them, and offering scholarships to likely youngsters. At that time it looked like a worth-while gamble for dividends in the distant future. It is now a pleasure to report that the gamble has come off much more quickly than anyone ever expected it would do.

There is not enough fuss made about this sort of thing in the newspapers. It is a fact that Scotland, which before the war had a reputation for solid craftsmanship and dull design, is now turning out the finest furniture in the world; that the world admits it and is buying on an international scale; and that the new reputation has been achieved in under three years. That, I feel, is something worth boasting about.

Not many firms in Scotland make furniture, so everything was easier than it might have been. They have been able to combine without too much difficulty. They have clubbed together and formed a company called the Scottish Furniture Manufacturers' Association, which draws on a common pool for design fees and, to some extent, marketing. Leading designers have been paid high fees for their work, and very good work it has been. Then, in 1950, the Association decided to plunge. It bought itself space at the British Industries Fair, spent a great deal of money on it, and then kept its fingers crossed.

The first word of the result came to me from an English architect I know, a canny soul. He drifted into my office one day looking slightly apprehensive and admitted that he'd lost his head on the opening day of the BIF and practically bought the stand. I began to look out for reports of the Fair in the English Press. In every one I read—literally without exception—this Scottish stand was mentioned as the outstanding exhibit in the whole exhibition. I have since met two members of the Association. They tell me they have booked orders from over forty different countries, and consider themselves launched on the international market on a big and solid scale.

They also tell me that they see no reason why the Scandinavians and the Italians should have the run of the new market in well-made and well-designed light-fittings which has grown up since the war. They have started now to see what they can do about it, working on the theory that there are few more horrible objects in any house either at home or abroad than the thing which hides the light bulb. I like the sound of this Association.

An attractive chair in cane and metal, produced by the Scottish National Institution for the War Blinded, which has sold well on the home market.

Postscript

CHRISTMAS presents are apt to be difficult when you have an American sister-in-law; but this year we had no trouble at all. Just as we were beginning, as usual, to wonder what we could possibly send to the land of plenty, we heard that over there they had started to collect (of all things) wally dugs. The demand so far exceeded the supply of the genuine Scottish article that factories in the States had actually started to manufacture them. Prices ranged from £10 to £15 a pair.

The pair we got cost ten bob in a Glasgow junk shop, and are now the pride of Beverley, Mass. All we need now is a cloakin' hen, and we're all set for next Christmas.

Dining-room furniture with wooden chairs, table and sideboard, made by a Glasgow firm specialising in up-to-date designs and catering for modern requirements.

Some examples of antique Scottish chinaware. Reading from left to right and top to bottom: A wally dug and wally cat, ever popular among Scots, dating from Victorian times; Scots fishwife (early nineteenth century); early Scottish pottery cat with characteristic marbling effect; an Edinburgh Volunteer (eighteenth century); a Portobello marriage bowl, showing a smiddy scene and the names of the newly-weds; an old Scots money box in the form of a hen on a nest.

Salvage

ABERDONIANS may disagree with me, but for many years it has been my impression that their Town Council knows what it is about. The snell east wind may keep it active, or it may simply be a coincidence; but it is a fact that whenever I visit the city to gather material for an article, the story I get is a success story. Naming no names, this is not so in all parts of Scotland. They have a brisk unsentimental way of doing things in Aberdeen, and the city is the better for it.

Their latest venture has been a long time a-coming (it has been a sore point with some citizens for forty years) but now that the job has been done it has been done quite exceptionally well. The one-time Cumberland Dwelling, where the Butcher slept on his way to Culloden and in recent years a slum of unmitigated squalor, has been put to rights and renamed Provost Skene's House after the man who built it in the seventeenth century.

When Her Majesty the Queen opened it recently she found a splendid mansion house with beautifully panelled walls and moulded ceilings, set in an open space which allowed its proportions to be seen. Before the restoration began it was an architectural wreck, hemmed in to its very walls by lesser wreckage and with its rooms chopped up into a warren of cubby-holes. Most of its present decorations had to be quarried out from behind layers of plaster and plywood; and it says much for the care with which this has been done that the work of the seventeenth century craftsmen has been discovered virtually intact. Surprisingly little had to be replaced. With great care, the veneer of squalor has been scraped away, revealing the old splendour underneath.

Provost Skene's house in Aberdeen, finely restored and again playing a part in the daily life of the " Silver City ". " Butcher " Cumberland slept here on his way to meet Prince Charles Edward's forces on Culloden Moor.

Restoration

ONE good deed in a wicked world has been the restoration, under the unlikely auspices of the Army, of a fine old house in Kirkcaldy. The house, which stands in Kirk Wynd and is over 300 years old, was bought three years ago as a recruiting office and handed to the Royal Engineers for repair. The Engineers went to work with a delicacy and imagination far beyond the call of duty and in a manner not laid down in Regulations. They delved into seventeenth century architecture, consulted the National Trust on the finer points, and even went to the Lord Lyon for the correct colours to be employed on the old cartouche over the door. The result is entirely admirable, a permanent asset to the town.

One associates the R.E.'s with Baillie bridges, demolitions and the lifting of mines, but it seems they are more versatile than we imagined. The present example of their skill is both unusual and impressive.

The house in Kirk Wynd, Kirkcaldy, restored by the Royal Engineers and now in use as a Regular Army Information Office.

The Old Tolbooth at the foot of the Royal Mile in Edinburgh, flanked by part of the spectacular restoration of the ancient thoroughfare, which is being carried out by Edinburgh Corporation.

A close-up of the Keep of Kellie Castle in Fife, which dates back to the mid fifteenth century.

Kellie Castle is an example of Scottish Baronial architecture at its most attractive. It was indeed fortunate that the castle stood untenanted between the thirties and seventies of last century, and was thus spared the possibility of "improvements" at a time when many fine old houses suffered from structural additions in an age of declining taste and false values. When the Castle did again become a family home it was finely restored by the new occupiers. Today it endures as one of the most impressive of all Scotland's historical houses.

High tea is an institution rather than a meal. A minister and his family take full advantage of it in a Princes Street (Edinburgh) tearoom during the annual General Assembly of the Church of Scotland.

Scots at Table

The Scottish High Tea

IN a changing world the Scottish high tea is holding its own, which only goes to show that Scotland knows a good thing when it sees one. Despite the war, the canning industry, and Philip Harben we still cling to our traditional diet, and cling to it so firmly that we formed a race apart when a National Food Survey Committee brought out its report. The figures were striking. It seems we eat 50 per cent. more cakes than any other part of Britain, and 30 per cent. more biscuits.

In less fortunate parts of these islands a tea is considered high if it includes a sausage or a bloater, but to the good Scot such things are a mere hors d'œuvre. We do not even set great store on the tea itself: we drink less of the stuff than they do in England. " High " to us means a little something solid and then getting down to the serious business of the day, which is cakes and pastries; and if anyone doubts this, let him consider the statistics for bread.

In England and Wales bread is mere stodge: here we use us our imagination. We like variety. We like rolls, and baps, and French bread to such an extent that while the average Briton eats 1·7 ounces of them every week, we eat no less than 9 ounces. It costs us more than ordinary bread, but we like to sample our way round the plates.

This trend, of course, reaches its peak when one arrives at the plate which in less civilised parts of the country is labelled " scones " and pronounced " scoanes ". It does not, as it does south of the Border, carry a few sad rock buns, but is only part of the spread. The Scots are not great cooks, but in this department they really do excel, as the list bears witness. It starts simply, with oatcakes and bannocks and girdle scones, builds up through pancakes, and scones of treacle and potato, to buns both iced and plain, gingerbread and shortbread; and there are variations on nearly all these themes. The Scottish high tea is a work of art, and if we knew our business we would make it a mainstay of the tourist trade instead of playing it down to afternoon tea level and following it with dinner. It is Scotland's only original contribution to cookery except the haggis, which few visitors try twice.

Digging a little deeper into the statistics, however, we find cause for alarm. Scots buy only 60 per cent. of the flour Englishmen buy, which suggests that much as they enjoy their baking they prefer to let the man in the shop do it for them. The man in the shop does it very well—the Edinburgh teashops, for example, are one of the attractions of the Festival —but it will be a bad day for the high tea when the housewife buys it in a bag. A nice light hand with scones has been a matter for pride as far back as anyone remembers, a thing which has given poise to hostesses for generations, and it would be a pity if we lost it.

The National Dish

A MILLER I know on Deeside makes a fair part of his income by grinding oats for porridge-connoisseurs. These people find that their palates are tickled by oats of a particular cut—special fine, perhaps, or No. 3, or No. 4½—and they take the trouble to write for a sack every now and then. He also finds that tastes vary from district to district, one preferring a smooth cut and another something more robust; and by catering for these tastes he prospers. To listen to him, the old legend of porridge-eating Scotland seems secure.

In fact it is not. The trade, becoming alarmed by the recent drop in sales, has been investigating our habits and has announced that we are eating only half the porridge we ate ten years ago. Indeed one delegate to a millers' conference has declared that in some districts of Scotland today only elderly people eat porridge regularly. Most of us skip the traditional first course at breakfast, and the rest prefer cereals.

Paradoxically, this should be a useful piece of evidence for those people who declare we are a better-fed nation than we were before the war. You need something solid to follow before you can abandon porridge and take to corn-flakes; and if half our porridge-eaters have been allowing the pot and the wooden spurtle to lie idle in the morning it can only mean that someone has been buying eggs, or bacon, or fish. These things were beyond the average working man's pocket before the war. It seems to me significant that he can now afford to throw overboard the finest piece of stodge on the market.

Above : a stage in the making of girdle scones with the finished product in the foreground.

Below : a table attractively laid for the traditional Scottish breakfast.

Mind you, he is missing something. It takes twenty minutes to make a real plate of porridge, but when you have it under your belt you can face the day with confidence. Wise men admittedly do top it off with something more solid (porridge has a habit of wearing off about eleven o'clock in the morning) but it provides a warm foundation and makes the bacon ration feel like a meal. Also it is nourishing, and hardy men have been bred on it. It is still the case in many country districts that no one bothers about tins if there is a sack of meal in the larder.

It is tempting to believe that we are abandoning our national dish because people have forgotten how to make it properly (I taste good porridge seldom in Scottish hotels, and in English ones never), but the answer is probably that people nowadays can afford to save time and sacrifice bulk with breakfast cereals. However, here is a recipe in case you feel like reviving a dying art and starting your day with the bland satisfaction which only porridge can give. Take a medium fistful of oat-meal per person and leave it to soak in a bowl overnight with just enough water to cover it. In the morning put twice as much water again in a pot, and when it is boiling pour in the contents of the bowl. Stir until the mixture boils, then leave it to simmer for twenty minutes. Salt to taste, and a Gaelic curse upon you if you use sugar.

This gives a smooth porridge, either thick or thin according to the amount of water you have used. For those who prefer something more vigorous, follow exactly the same method and recipe, but do not leave the meal to soak overnight. Tip it, mixed with cold water, straight into the boiling pot.

The true artist sprinkles dry meal into a pot and disdains to moisten it first, but this creates pitfalls for the beginner. Dry meal can cause lumps, and lumps can cure a man of porridge for life. I once knew a woman who liked them, indeed chewed them, but it turned out she liked the skin on top of cocoa as well.

From top to bottom: Scottish lobsters ready to serve in an Edinburgh restaurant; a salmon from a Highland river after an Edinburgh chef has finished with it—and before the diners-out have begun; oatcakes, mealy puddings, and a breakfast roll. Finally, on the right, a Scottish chef with that incomparable dish—the haggis.

A Matter of Taste

SOME misconceptions would have to be overcome by the Ayr canning firm which tried to popularise a taste for mackerel. To my mind mackerel shares with venison the top place for the most misunderstood British food. Both are excellent, but there have been times when it has been impossible even to give them away.

The folk-tale that mackerel are unclean feeders is absolute nonsense. They are clean and vigorous fish, firm-fleshed and of a heartening yet delicate flavour not unlike herring, and when taken fresh and either fried in oatmeal or grilled make a splendid dish. I have not tasted them canned, but I should imagine they would be something like tunny. They can be caught almost anywhere off the west coast during the summer months, and the idea of someone trying to make a go of them appeals to me. We are far too conservative in our food, and especially in our fish. Haddock is all very well, but there is no need to live on it.

As for venison, even years of war failed to remove the misconceptions which surround it, and the end of meat rationing knocked the bottom clean out of the market. Once more a noble dish is neglected. People still think it is stringy, strongly-flavoured, and tough.

Allow me to tell you something about venison. The bullock bred for beef spends its life wandering about a field doing practically nothing but sleep and eat, and the amount of really tender steak it produces in a lifetime of ease is not more than a few pounds. The stag, on the other hand, has to work for its living, eats coarse stuff that would choke a sheep, and spends much of its time dashing madly up and down mountains; yet the entire haunch of a stag is as tender as butter. The evil reputation of venison is, I am convinced, due to the quaint idea that to cook it one must hack it into chunks, fling it in a pot, and boil it to shreds under the pretence of making stew.

This idea is mistaken, unless one is dealing with the forequarters, and the forequarters of a very old stag at that. There have been times when I have lived on venison, and I assure you that if you have the good fortune to acquire a cut off the haunch you can treat it as steak, even to the extent of frying or grilling it. Futhermore, the ribs can be roasted. The meat is darker than beef, but it is tender and delicious.

As for stag's liver . . . but in the city you will probably never have the luck to taste that: we keep it here in the country.

Heavy taxation after the Union of English and Scottish Parliaments forced a decline in the wine-drinking tradition among Scotsmen, who formerly carried on immense trade with France. Something of it still remained in the time of early nineteenth century artist Walter Geikie, whose print called " Peace and Plenty " shows something of the pleasure in wine after a hard day's work.

The Return to Claret

PORRIDGE may be going, but the Scottish table is again graced by something which had departed from it for close on two centuries. Claret, once as popular in this country as whisky, is back.

The economics of drinking today are such that most of our native tipple is exported, or sold at home with an inordinate tax clapped upon it; and the French and other nations have seen their chance and have taken it. They have exported in their turn vast quantities of the cheaper wines. Many people, seeing the choice between one bottle of whisky and four bottles of tolerable wine (or five bottles if your palate, like mine, is not too fussy) have decided that wine is something they can afford to drink if they can afford to drink at all. As a result our consumption of it has nearly trebled in three years. Women, on the whole, still like it sweet; but the men are buying claret again. Ghostly heads are no doubt being nodded approvingly in the rookeries along the Royal Mile.

Our importers are taking note of the trend, with strange results in the wine-shops. The basis of the swing has obviously been financial, so the markets of the world have been scraped for cheap wines which are drinkable. Some of the results have been happy, and some not: a visit to the wine merchant by a man who can't spend more than seven or eight shillings a bottle can be an interesting gamble, because the merchant is sometimes as much at sea with the exotics as his customers are. Lately we have seen claret from Chile (and perfectly drinkable it was, too, though my first bottle was pushed across the counter to me rather diffidently with the warning that for all anyone knew it was red ink), a series of peculiar hocks from Yugoslavia, and a Sauterne from, of all places, Spain. There is a perpetual rumour that someone has discovered a good hock at six-and-sixpence and an Empire burgundy that doesn't taste of syrup of figs, but no one can ever find them. There is growing up a class of people who are not wine snobs, but bargain hunters.

The admiration of visitors for distinctive Scottish food and delicacies have caused Scots to look with new eyes at what they had hitherto regarded as normal everyday fare. Above is a selection of better known Scottish dainties now being exported to many countries outside Scotland.

Berwick Cockles have appealed to Scotland's palates since the original firm began to make them in 1801.

Jethart Snails are made from a secret recipe passed down from family to family. They were introduced over a century ago by a French prisoner-of-war working for a Jedburgh baker.

Once known as "Soor Plooms," the Braw Lads of Gala Water give their nickname to a famous Scottish sweet now sold all over the country.

A commodity eagerly sought after by visitors to Scotland's Capital—Edinburgh Rock.

Souvenir of every Scotsman's childhood: "strippit balls".

Scotland's Sweet Tooth

SCOTLAND has a sweet tooth. The variety alone proves that. Berwick Cockles, Jethart Snails, Soor Plooms, Edinburgh Rock—these are the favourite "sweeties" of every Scotsman's childhood. Today there are over 1,000 sweet-makers in Scotland, catering for a national public which consumes, on an average, seven ounces of confectionery per head per week. Exports are huge: Americans and Canadians can get quite sentimental over strippit balls, granny sookers, Helensburgh toffee and extra-strong Scotch mint sent to them in handsome tartan packages.

Another favourite delicacy: Russian toffee.

Black bun, shortbread, nuts and a whisky decanter on a Scottish sideboard at the end of any year—when the festivities of Yule and the " Daft Days" of Hogmanay celebration make for an enjoyable interlude in the depths of winter.

In the United Services Museum at Edinburgh Castle are these statuettes showing uniforms of various Scottish Regiments at the time of Waterloo. From left to right these are: Officers of the Royal North British Dragoons (Scots Greys); 79th (Cameron) Highlanders; 71st (Highland Light Infantry); 42nd (Black Watch); Sergeant, 92nd (Gordon) Highlanders; Officers, 93rd (Sutherland) Highlanders; and 78th (2nd Seaforth) Highlanders. Opposite page—one of R. R. McIan's fanciful prints showing a McNiel clansman in warlike array.

Scots at War

A Distinguished Warrior

I HAVE pleasant memories of Dr. George Pratt Insh, that most charming scholar and historian whose death in 1956 was deeply regretted. Dr. Insh was an authority on Scottish colonial history, a gentle and kindly soul who could not possibly have had an enemy in the whole wide world yet who conceived it to be his duty to serve in both World Wars. He fought in the first and tried to do so again in the second, when he was approaching sixty, but was diverted into the Army Education Corps.

It was there that I met him after a lapse of years, in a building in Wakefield which commanded a fine view of the prison. It was the headquarters of the Corps, and to it was haled every now and then a contingent of officers to undergo a course of instruction. There were many silly courses during the war, but this one was in a class by itself. The Corps had existed before the war, when its members had run what were in effect schools in the peacetime headquarters of the regiments. Now, in 1942 with the Germans just across the Channel, there was no place for it. However, every branch of the army seemed to be running a course, so the Education Corps ran one too. I was one of a batch of thirty officers who turned up to be taught, in a fortnight, how to educate a battalion which had neither the time nor the desire to be educated. It was the most fatuous course I ever attended.

In the middle of it, a senior instructor, was Major Pratt Insh. The army had put him there, so he was making the best of it. I have to thank him for a delightful series of lectures delivered with a straight face and the greatest erudition on subjects which had nothing whatever to do with military education. If Major Insh could not educate the army, then he would educate us. He did so for a fortnight. It was memorable.

It was done very simply. For example, one day he said: " The subject this morning, gentlemen, is . . . er . . . let me see . . . yes, ' How to Prepare a Lecture.' "

He looked mildly round his class, and with a twinkle in his eye continued: " How to prepare a lecture. Now an excellent subject to prepare a lecture about, gentlemen, would be the Roman Wall, which passes not so very far north of here. The Wall was built . . ."

And away he went for half an hour on the Roman Occupation. It was fascinating and, as he well knew, of no military value. It was one of the earlier war crimes that this amiable and distinguished man should have been wasting his time on the likes of us instead of preparing some part of the war's history, the work he was trained to do. In the end he did it.

In 1945 he accepted an invitation from the director of the historical section of the War Cabinet to help in the preparation of the official history of the Civil Defence Services.

Yet he carried off that Wakefield business with an air. Lesser men would have been crushed by the stupidity of the thing. He put his tongue in his cheek and proceeded to create his own small corner of civilisation out of intractable material.

Combat Vignette

WHEN the old Highland Division was forced to lay down its arms at St. Valery-en-Caux in 1940, it fought until it could fight no more and then mounted a spit-and-polish parade. It marched into captivity with boots as clean as St. Valery's supply of blacking would allow.

When the new Highland Division liberated St. Valery in 1944, it happened that the battalion in which I served was the first to reach the town (for the record, a Glasgow subaltern called Jerry Dawson was the first man in) and there it was possible to see how the Germans had spent their last days before withdrawing. As nearly every billet had empty bottles strewn over the floor, we could believe the local story that most of them, officers and men, had been drunk for a week before they left.

In my own billet I found a case of empty bottles which remains in my mind as the most vivid picture in all that memorable day—more vivid even than my colonel finding his old wrecked trucks in the ditches and crooning over his old company sign, produced by a farmer who had kept it hidden for four years because, he said, he had known the colonel would come back for it. This case contained bottles of Benedictine from the factory at Fécamp, a few miles down the road; and the bottles were sample ones. Each had contained only a thimbleful of liquor. I counted them. There were over two hundred. The room was littered with tiny corks.

I like to think of that German, alone in the little bare room, with the Allied advance rolling over the Seine towards him and no hope in his heart at all, trying to get drunk. Did he draw twenty little corks, empty the bottles into a glass, and have a proper drink? I don't think so. He sat there and drank the bottles one at a time, one sip from each, on and on for hours, thorough even in his cups. It must have been a singularly dreary proceeding. It has always seemed to me a fitting end to the German occupation of St. Valery.

An officer of the Royal Scots Greys (2nd Dragoons), the famous Scottish Cavalry Regiment which bears the proud motto "Second to None". The Regiment was formed at the Binns, West Lothian, in 1678, under Lieutenant-General Thomas Dalziel and Lord Charles Murray. It includes Blenheim, Ramillies, Oudenarde and Malplaquet among the famous battles in its early history, and its fallen are commemorated by the well-known equestrian statue in Princes Street, Edinburgh.

Fleur-de-lys lace in blue and white adorns the chests of drummers of the Guards Regiments. Buttons in groups of three show that the man above is in the Scots Guards.

A side drum of the Argyll and Sutherland Highlanders, showing the cords used to tighten the skins and the decorative plaited loops.

The elaborate trappings of a Drum Major of the Gordon Highlanders.

National Servicemen

AFTER having spent the first few months of the war in the H.L.I. trying to keep step with small, square citizen-soldiers whose waists appeared to be about knee-high, I am not surprised to learn from the Medical Research Council that the men of Clydeside are the smallest in Britain. The only wonder is (you cannot conceive what the Light Infantry pace is like) that they are not smaller. According to the figures recently published the average young man living in Glasgow, Paisley and Mother-well is 66.7 inches high, which means that the average Highlander can give him 1.1 inches and the average Briton .8 of an inch. It used to feel a lot more than that to me.

An inch of difference takes some accounting for, and it cannot be put down to environment. The figures, which cover the whole of Britain, were based on measurements taken during the medical examination of National Servicemen. National Servicemen come from every city and every class of society; and since Glasgow has no more slums than, say, Liverpool, its place at the bottom of the list is puzzling. One can only conclude that heredity is at the root of it.

At this point one man's guess becomes as good as another, because a racial trend capable of producing so great a difference must go back a very long way indeed and there are plenty of races in our blood to choose from. One theory goes back to the Neolithic Age. It holds that people of the " Mediterranean " race (some of whom are known to have reached Scotland in Neolithic times) have shown themselves in other countries to be particularly adaptable to new conditions, such as mechanical engineering and slums. The Mediterranean people were short and dark, as indeed were my pace-makers in the H.L.I.

In times of emigration (more than a million Scots have emigrated in the past century) the Mediterraneans would happily adapt themselves to the Machine Age at home while their more countrified neighbours went overseas. Hence the number of short dark people in Glasgow.

Well. . . . This theory is subscribed to by at least one American professor, and I noticed the *Glasgow Herald* airing it again the other day. It sounds a bit far-fetched to me. I'm all for playing safe and blaming the Picts.

The Pipe Major (left) belongs to The Black Watch, Royal Highland Regiment of Canada—a Montreal corps. A drummer of the Argyll and Sutherland Highlanders turns his sporran onto his hip so that it will not interfere with the drum.

A drummer of (left) the Coldstream Guards, and a Drum Major of the Scots Guards.

The Pipes and Drums of the Black Watch on parade in West Berlin. The regiment recently completed a tour of duty in Germany as part of the British Army of the Rhine.

Nights on the Orne

THE fallacy, widely believed in Scotland, that the mosquito is a creature of the tropics is natural enough because it is an extremely rare insect in this country; but the idea has few supporters in Coatbridge. In Coatbridge they know better. With the breeding grounds of Gartcosh and the Monkland Canal inside easy dive-bombing range they know by experience that the pleasures of the midnight hunt with slipper or rolled-up newspaper are not reserved for Africans or Indians. So fierce, in fact, have *theobaldia annulata* and *taeniorhyncus richiardii* become that the town once set aside an annual £280 to rid itself of the scourge.

The news of this was considered sufficiently unusual to warrant headlines in the newspapers, but it came as no surprise to one-time members of the Highland and Lowland Divisions, both of which were once eaten alive in unlikely places both geographical and physiological. The Lowland Division had its baptism of fire no farther afield than Colchester early in the war. The H.D. had to wait until later—much later than might be imagined when one considers that they made their name in Africa. Mosquitoes were almost never seen in the desert; and even in Sicily, where malaria casualties were more than twice as numerous as battle casualties, there was nothing that a handful of midges could not have bettered any wet afternoon at Crianlarich. On its return for D-Day the Division was even inclined to be cocky about it when questioned by anxious relatives.

It learned about the mosquito, not in Africa or Sicily, but in France alongside its Lowland comrades. Much was written at the time about the horrors of the bridgehead, but for some reason (possibly because at that period they seldom slept in trenches) the war correspondents barely mentioned the mosquito. It caused more lack of sleep than ever the German gunners did, produced a score of stings on the back of each hand of each soldier each night, and planted in the minds of 30,000 Scotsmen the ineradicable conviction that the most bloodthirsty mosquito on earth inhabited the valley of the Orne. It still makes me itch to think of it.

Coatbridge would do well to persevere with its spraying and smoking, since the only other inexpensive cure is no longer available. Once it was simple and effective. You dug a slit-trench, roofed in all but a small entrance, and then captured two Germans. Over the entrance you stretched their cellular-weave underpants—a fact which explains why, in times of stress when operations were hurried, so many of our late enemies arrived at the prisoner-of-war cage in their shirt-tails.

Bottles and Reminiscences

BOTTLES are evocative things when found in foreign lands, and many a scene of battle now remains in our minds as " the place where we found the brandy " when less pleasant features of the day have faded. That is the way soldiers' minds work.

Leading the raconteurs are members of the Guards Armoured Division. No one can cap their story. It was they who investigated a warehouse on the right of the road as you go north from Eindhoven to Nijmegen and discovered there a German hoard of half a million bottles of champagne. Even so, others (the Highland Division among them) did themselves well in a more modest way. I myself have pleasant memories of liberating the Benedictine factory at Fécamp. There was also the glorious evening, when as Le Havre fell and the last shot was fired, ten weary private soldiers and one lance-corporal from the county of Caithness found themselves at the door of an officers' mess from which the enemy had lately fled. I saw it myself. It was by a road which ran through a wood. They dragged a table to the grassy verge, set upon it a clean white cloth and many bottles, and celebrated the victory. When (as happened often) a car passed, the corporal rose from his seat, stopped the car, and invited the driver to join them for a moment or two. It was all done with dignity, and a complete disregard for rank. It stands to the everlasting credit of one brigadier (I tell you, I saw it myself) that he not only accepted the invitation and sat in the place of honour on the lance-corporal's right, but proposed a toast (" To all acting lance-corporals, unpaid ") before he drove on again.

Then again there was Algerian wine at three-ha'pence a pint, and Sicilian stuff at nothing at all, and the little man in Hamburg who, until his clients started to reach the hospitals, made up any liqueur on earth if you gave him the labels. My own most cherished experience is, however, of a quieter sort. After Alamein my unit stopped, exhausted, to reorganise, and that night I found four things—a packet of German nightlights, the spring seats from an Italian truck, two gallons of chianti, and a dug-out quarried into the sand beneath a Mark IV tank. It was dark by five, so for a whole week we had nothing to do but go to bed at night. We had not seen beds for a long time. I lay on springs under twenty tons of steel with a cup on one hand, and the lights on the other, reading *Wuthering Heights*; and in all my life I have never been happier.

Official Photograph   Crown Copyright

Major-General Douglas M. Wimberley, C.B., D.S.O., M.C., Commander of the Highland Division during the North African campaign, and known affectionately to all who served under him as " Big Tam, King of Scotland ".

The King of Scotland

OF all the examples of what modern jargon calls reconversion, and what in a former age was known as beating swords into ploughshares, the one that pleased me most was the new Principal of University College, Dundee, in the University of St. Andrews, shortly after the last war.

He was then known to the country at large as Major-General D. M. Wimberley, C.B., D.S.O., M.C.; but to some 15,000 members and ex-members of the Highland Division he will never be anything else but Big Tam, King of Scotland.

In the Western Desert, Big Tam was a legend; but in spite of all his exploits (he had a habit of having jeeps shot from under him) the one which probably brought most success to his men was his astute appreciation of the part played in battle by morale. Morale is a delicate flower, and it has to be cultivated. Big Tam's methods were unique.

In the early days it was difficult to inculcate *esprit de corps* into anything so big as a division—men were apt to think first and last of their own battalion—but he was equal to the problem. As soon as the 51st landed in Africa H.D. signs sprouted everywhere. The men wore them on their shoulders, they were on every vehicle, there was an H.D. Track (in the end it stretched all the way from Alamein to Tunisia) signposted with monstrous H.D.'s every few hundred yards. It was even said Tam wore them on his pyjamas. Though the Division had never fired a shot in anger and there was no means of knowing how it would fare in its first action, he insisted that it should advertise itself. The policy paid enormous dividends. The Jocks joked about it at first. Some officers wondered if, should the Division do badly when action came, they would ever hold up their heads again. Then came Alamein, and success. After that the Jocks were so offensively Highland Division that they plastered H.D.'s on every vacant wall for two thousand miles and were known to the rest of the Eighth Army as the Highway Decorators. Morale went high and stayed there.

He also held the theory that the Division would fight its best if it contained the maximum number of Scotsmen, and to this end he sent a captain to Suez. The only job this officer had to do was shanghai Scotsmen from every boatload of reinforcements that docked and whip them up the desert before the proper authorities realised they had been robbed.

The finely modelled head of the staff carried by the Bugle Major of the Highland Light Infantry. The elephant commemorates the regiment's prowess at the battle of Assaye in 1803. The H.L.I. was one of the Scottish regiments threatened with loss of identity through amalgamation with another regiment in an announcement made in 1957.

Scots became an obsession with him. I remember being at his headquarters one day and seeing him emerge from his office-truck and depart in his jeep. The customary escort of two military policemen on motorbikes drove after him. Ten seconds later a perspiring Provost Marshal ran into the open, waving his arms and shouting.

" Who went with the General? " he yelled.

" Ramsbotham and Jenkins, sir."

The major moaned. " In the name of heaven! Get them back. Go after them! " He turned to the dug-out inhabited by the provost section. " McDonald! " he yelled. " McGregor! "

University College, Dundee? Yes, a most interesting appointment.

A modern Scottish equivalent of a gold mine: a Highland distillery at Dalwhinnie, near the Inverness-shire-Perthshire border.

The Water of Life

The production of what is known outside Scotland as " Scotch " is heavily controlled and regulated. Here the resident Customs Officer at a Highland distillery takes a sample of fermenting liquid for testing.

ALL sorts of fanciful figures are given for the value of the whisky produced each year on the island where I live, the Isle of Islay; but it can safely be put at not less than £2,000,000, and that does not include duty. It gives some idea of the importance whisky has acquired in the economy, not just of Islay or even of Scotland, but the whole of Britain. Whisky is Britain's number one dollar earner, and so earnestly is it sought after abroad that we have the greatest difficulty in finding enough for ourselves to drink.

Most of the big distilleries started about a hundred years ago, or a little over that. At the close of the eighteenth century it was mainly something one made at the bottom of the garden, for there were few Highland communities without at least one still, and most had several. It cost next to nothing.

Then the excisemen conducted a series of blitzes around the countryside, and within fifty years the private still had practically vanished. Illicit stills kept going, but on nothing like their former wholesale scale. Small distilleries started up under licence to fill the deeply-felt need. Most of them were quite small, about the size of a fairly big house. Indeed, my neighbour on Islay lives in a house which was one of these small distilleries.

The final stage came when the illicit still was virtually stamped out; and the distilling business, in the natural way of things, became bigger and bigger until the present-day large establishments arose, often with their own private piers and harbours, and certainly surrounded with the long low shapes of the bond warehouses.

The heart of Scotch whisky, the thing that makes it Scotch, is the straight malt liquor supplied by these Highland distilleries. Once it was the heart and body too; but early in the present century the distillers began to blend the malt whisky of the Highlands with grain whisky made elsewhere, the result being all the popular brand names we know today. The blends caught on and are now drunk the world over. They have a lighter look and flavour to them than the old malts.

Yet many, myself included, prefer the single malts to the modern blends. There is an oiliness to them, a heavy body, which goes well with peaty water; and they have great character. I was delighted to hear recently that some of our local stuff, bottled straight, is finding a connoisseur's market in America and is selling at a higher price than usual, like a vintage wine.

Even so, popularity has its drawbacks. We produce hundreds of thousands of gallons of the real Mackay on this island and make lots of lovely dollars, but just you try to buy a bottle round about New Year time. The place is bulging with the stuff, but you can't buy a dram for love nor money.

Part of the complicated, age-old process of whisky making: wet barley is spread out on the malting floor, allowed to germinate, and then dried off in a kiln. Smoke from peat fires helps to give Highland malt whisky its distinctive flavour. Below: Whisky production would also seem to be taken in deadly earnest by those actually on the job. The liquid is kept moving while the Exciseman measures the specific gravity.

Scots and
their Music

Gaeldom's Crowning Hour

ONE cannot hold a party involving several thousands of people when the tourist season is cramming the hotels, so the legend of the dour Highlander will probably continue to die hard. October is the month when he lets his hair down and enjoys himself, and by then the visitors have gone home to tell their friends about the grave, phlegmatic people they have met. They never see the antic Highlander who descends upon the hotels and boarding-houses when the last visitor has gone and the time has come for the Mod.

The Mod, which in 1953 celebrated its Golden Jubilee at Oban, is to Scotland what the Eisteddfod is to Wales, an annual party loosely draped round a singing and versifying competition. It draws competitors and their supporters from all parts of the Highlands and from those parts of the Lowlands where Highlanders have settled, and it comes as the climax of a process which has been gradually whipping up enthusiasm since the spring.

For example, in the village where I live, the school was closed one day in May because everyone had hived off to the nearest small town to take part in what one might call the preliminary heats of the Mod. The winners have since been practising, closely criticised by the rest of us; and when the great day comes in the second week of October, something like a couple of hundred of us will cram on to the boat to sustain them on their way and impress the judges with our applause. So enthusiastic are we that we shall even be prepared to sit in a hall for an entire morning or afternoon and listen with every appearance of pleasure to a dozen choirs all singing the same piece one after the other.

But the singing is the least of it. It is only the excuse. The Mod is a social occasion, a gigantic party which begins in the boats, buses and trains, ends in the small hours of the last day, and has something in it for everybody. There are high jinks for the youngsters, learned discussions for their elders, and the exciting atmosphere of a town gone completely Gaelic in a night. Much is said. A certain amount of the native drink is consumed. It is the crowning hour of the Gaelic movement, and it is completely and utterly successful.

Our Dance Music

I HOPE that in the middle of all the Arts we are promised every summer at the Edinburgh Festival a place is found for one which, even if it does not quite aspire to a capital letter, is peculiarly Scottish and thoroughly festive. I mean Scottish dance music, now enjoying a vogue which bears all the signs of being permanent, and yet which does not seem to have found much of a niche in any official Festival programme.

I am an addict. I admit it freely. I like these ancient, cheery, unassuming tunes, and I admire the ingenuity which is being lavished today on arranging them. There are at least a couple of dozen bands in this country which can play them not only with precision but with wit; and I count it as one of the few great things the B.B.C. has done for Scotland that these national tunes have been saved from semi-oblivion and put in the forefront of popular taste. They are more popular on the air than jazz; and that, considering that jazz is not only a habit but an industry, is astonishing.

Gaily designed gramophone record covers like these indicate that the Scots and their music are appreciated in many countries outside Scotland. The voices of these two popular Scots singing stars are sent to overseas enthusiasts on long-playing gramophone records.

It seems to me, too, that they should have an export value. They are distinctively Scottish. They are like nothing else in the world, except perhaps early American and Canadian " barn dance " music, which they probably influenced. They are a taste so easily acquired that the feet start tapping before the tune has registered on the mind. They are good of their kind, because they represent the winnowings of several centuries. And they are fun.

Other countries have done more with their folk-music. German *lieder* have been sung round the world and have helped to make many a continental holiday. I have seen tourists cramming Swiss pubs to hear the local choir, and I have been deaved deaf by allegedly Tzigane orchestras no farther off from home than Sauchiehall Street. In the Tyrol, gentlemen in leather trousers make a good thing of it, in the season.

I cannot help feeling that if we knew our business the fiddle and the concertina would have been roped in long ago to help the tourist trade, and our guests would have been sent home whistling. This year the opportunity is exceptional. It is not trash we have to offer, served up for the occasion, but a living and ancient tradition so acceptable that a million Scots can tune in to it from choice, for the sheer pleasure of hearing the beat, and the tune, and the twiddly bits.

It is a pity we don't play in our pubs. Three bars on the harmonium and trumpet can bring up a Paris cafe as large as life. We have something as evocative at home, and we use it only for ourselves. It's downright selfish.

Left: A solitary piper on the shore of Loch Awe, Argyllshire, plays the instrument and music traditional to his surroundings.

Kirkintilloch Children's Choir is one of Scotland's most famous groups of young singers. This young member is taking part in a broadcast which may bring letters from as far apart as Jamaica and Murmansk.

The Pibroch

ONE of the more dubious statements by Scotsmen was that once made by Mr. Seumas MacNeill, joint principal of the College of Piping. "Anyone who enjoys classical music," he said, "will enjoy the classical music of the pipes—the pibroch. Only those who have never heard the pibroch condemn the pipes as being 'a lot of noise.'"

That is a fine upstanding statement, but I doubt if it is true. The war gave me an excellent chance to study reactions to the pipes (I remember with particular pleasure the stupefaction of two camels at Beni Yuissef), and although I agree that most people did not dismiss them out of hand as a lot of noise I feel the word " enjoy " is perhaps too strong.

More than that, I altogether disagree that classical piping as opposed to the simpler marches, strathspeys and reels is likely to appeal to the uninitiated. The *piob mhor* is hard work. Even the English can soon disentangle the tune from simple piping, but the *piob mhor* grows slowly on the ear, and while it is doing so it is like the singing of my friend John Methuen, of whom it was said that his voice did not go up and down but only got louder and softer. In fact, I am prepared to go as far as to say that for the first few times of hearing, the *piob mhor* is completely bewildering to those whose musical education has taken place in quieter surroundings.

I myself learned it the hard way. At the beginning of the war I was stationed in a castle with a battalion whose officers held three mess nights every week. The mess was tiny, and panelled to the ceiling in oak. Three times a week the Pipe-Major came in after the port and for seventeen minutes by the clock gave us " The Terrible Battle ", squeezing round and round the table in the narrow gap between the backs of the chairs and the wall. He played it, I now realise, extremely well; but in that oaken box, with the cutlery leaping on the table and one's gastric juices wrestling with brown stew, the sweat used to stand on my brow. Even so, I came in time to enjoy the pibroch, though only after we had moved to less cramped quarters.

The best pibroch ever I heard was " Lament for the Children ", played before a group of wondering Sicilian peasants who clearly made nothing of it at all; but the most impressive was in Tunisia. We were camped on the edge of the cork forest, with the Mediterranean far below, and I had invited an English friend to dine with me. We were sitting in the open

at dusk, drinking wine at tuppence-ha'penny a pint, when sounds of tuning pipes arose on the evening air; and the Pipie, who had a beard down to here, came striding out of the forest like the wrath of God playing " The Glen is Mine ". It was almost dark at the time. We were suspended between the mountains and the sea. The man looked enormous as he circled round, the music swelling and receding. It was the most glorious noise I have ever heard.

My friend sat with his mouth open, his wine seeping away unheeded in the grass. " Can such things be! " he said, and I thought that at last I had found a Sassenach with an ear ready made. " Can such things be! " he said again. " How long did it take him to grow that beard? "

With a Hidrum-Hodrum

THERE are few things more impressive than the enthusiast in the grip of his subject. There is fire even in the bridge-addict as he explains how he finessed the jack, and the golfer recounting his round has all the thunder of waves beating on a distant shore. But where pipe-majors are involved, enthusiasm verges upon megalomania. Pipe-majors are a race apart, men of single purpose and a distant eye, dedicated to the memorising, teaching, and playing of a thousand tunes. They have a commanding presence and a great dignity. They fix their classes with their eye, raise their hands, say: " One, two. With a hidrum-hodrum," and the chanters bleat as if all the snakes of India were being charmed. Oh, they are most serious-minded men, the pipe-majors.

Not so the fiddlers. Fiddlers are less stern, though they play the same tunes. Perhaps it is because they know that, should memory fail, they can always use a sheet of music, a thing no piper can ever do; or it may just be that fiddling is more restful. However, you must not fall into the error of believing that, because of this difference, the fiddlers are any less enthusiastic than the pipers. They are not. They are tarred with the same brush—a fanatical love of the music of Scotland and a desire to play it on the slightest provocation.

Hence the strathspey and reel societies. They are made up of people whose pleasure it is to play, and play well, those heady, feet-catching tunes which most of us associate with village dances, tunes which in many cases go back hundreds of years. The best-known societies are those of Edinburgh, Glasgow, Aberdeen, Inverness, and Oban; and some idea of the size and quality of their following may be gathered from the fact that when the Glasgow Society holds its annual gathering it not only packs the St. Andrew's Halls but so works upon the emotions of its audience that there is always dancing in the corridors before the night is out. Good Glaswegian though I am, I must admit it is no ordinary music that allows a man to forget his surroundings to such an extent that he hoochs in the St. Andrew's Halls.

It might be as well at this stage to explain what strathspeys and reels are, and wherein their difference lies. They are the dance-music of Scotland, both Highland and Lowland; for, although the present-day societies are mainly Highland, although the tunes are played on the pipes as well as the fiddle, and although many of them have Gaelic words, they were once danced to and sung as far south as Carlisle and began to wane only when the waltz and the polka came over from the Continent a hundred-odd years ago. They usually consist of two measures of four bars each, and each measure is repeated. A reel takes fifteen seconds to play through, a strathspey anything from twenty to twenty-four seconds. But their lilt defies accurate description. Everyone knows a reel when he hears it. For a strathspey, think of the ancient " Miller's Wedding " and " Mrs. Hamilton of Wishaw ". You probably know them better under the titles Burns gave them—" Auld Lang Syne " and " My love is like a red, red rose ".

The history of strathspeys and reels is long and so wrapped up in adaptation, evolution, and downright piracy that modern experts still come to blows about it. The first composer of whom any reliable record survives was born in 1675, and was hanged in 1700 by a long-suffering public. His name was James Macpherson, a brigand to trade and one-time business associate of Rob Roy. While awaiting execution, he composed that still-popular tune " Macpherson's Rant ". He played it on the scaffold, held out his fiddle to the mob and offered it to anyone who would keep it for his sake, and, when no one would accept it, broke it over the executioner's head and threw himself off the ladder.

It was 1750 before the music publishers took up the reels, and by then many of them were so old that the composers were unknown. The tune

Pipe Major R. Crabb, B.E.M., of the Scots Guards against a background of Highland hills. Martial music takes a high place in Scotland's musical tradition.

The martial music of the Gael is heard to good effect in historical, open-air settings, as at the Military Tattoo on the esplanade of Edinburgh Castle. Below: gentler music accompanies an eighteenth century dance in period costume on a Scottish stage.

we now know as " Auld Lang Syne " was in the first collection ever published. No one knows where it came from, or who composed it.

Then reels and strathspeys became not only popular, but fashionable. Niel Gow, the greatest fiddler of them all, and probably the greatest that ever lived, was taken up by the nobility. Burns, who knew him, began to adapt and rewrite the lyrics.

Jazz has killed most of that in the cities now; and, except where the societies flourish, one must, to see the fiddler hold his own again, go to that kind of country dance where elderly gentlemen carry two spare collars. The pipers play their part in keeping the tradition alive, especially those of the Highland regiments. I have seen Sicilian peasants walk for miles to cheer at " Caber Feidh ", one of the oldest tunes of them all; and on one memorable occasion saw camels watching with a wild amaze while reels were practised at 6 a.m. below the Pyramids. The old songs get around.

Still, of late they have been more than holding their own against the saxophone. Thanks largely to the B.B.C. the societies are now reaching greater audiences, and the popularity of these broadcasts is encouraging them to a new high-level of skill. They know that as soon as they reach a certain standard there is time waiting for them on the air. They also know that Hugh M'Phee of the Gaelic department, a strathspey enthusiast himself, has a sympathetic ear when it comes to discussing new orchestrations and new programmes. And I never saw a strathspey and reel society that needed any encouragement in any case.

The broadcasts are good. The meetings of the societies are better. The annual gatherings of the societies are terrific. But best of all is a village hall I know, the kind of little hall where the old tunes have been kept alive since long before my lifetime and they dance such things as Brown's Reel, and Draps o' Brandy, and never think of starting with anything else but the Circassian Circle. The night of the Games is the best night to go. There's a wee chap with the fiddle, and another with a harmonium. And, man, that fiddler is good.

BOOK NOW for your SCOTTISH TOUR

Completely inclusive of meals and Hotel accommodation, the Extended Tours operated by the Group offer the finest way to see the country at reasonable cost.

TOURS from LONDON

Extended Tours from 6 to 16 days to the far north, from £22 10 0.

Also Express Luxury Service to Edinburgh and Glasgow, fare 40s. Single ; or 2-Day Service to Edinburgh, £12 7 6 Return, £6 5 0 Single (inclusive of meals and hotels), and a new 3-Day Service to Edinburgh including meals and hotels £10 10 0 Single.

TOURS from EDINBURGH

A large choice of Extended Tours from 3 to 13 days covering the whole of Scotland, English Lakes, Welsh Mountains and Devon and Cornwall, from £8 10 0. Also 40 Day Tours.

TOURS from GLASGOW

Extended Tours to the farthest north and the romantic north-west, from £7 0 0. Also numerous Day Tours to Scotland's famous beauty spots.

TOURS from INVERNESS

Extended coach tours to the far north, from approx. £3 9 0, and 24 Day Tours cover as far north as John o' Groat's, west to the Isle of Skye, and down to Royal Deeside.

Write for tours literature to any of the Companies or to the Group's London Office.

Scottish Bus Group

SCOTTISH OMNIBUSES LTD
45 Princes Street, Edinburgh   Phone : WAV 2 5 1 5

W. ALEXANDER & SONS LTD
473 Cathedral Street, Glasgow   Phone : DOUglas 6 3 4 1-6

DAVID LAWSON LTD
Coach Station, Dundas Street, Glasgow   Phone : DOUglas 3 3 5 5

WESTERN SMT CO LTD
290 Buchanan Street, Glasgow   Phone : DOUglas 8 6 3 4-5

HIGHLAND OMNIBUSES LTD
Farraline Park, Inverness   Phone : 1 8 1 6

LONDON ADDRESS ALL COMPANIES: 298 REGENT STREET   **Phones LANgham 4708: MUSeum 9373-4-5**

A BREAKFAST FAVOURITE THE WORLD OVER

GOLDEN SHRED
puts the taste on the toast

JAMES ROBERTSON & SONS, Preserve Manufacturers, **LTD., PAISLEY**
Factories also at LONDON, MANCHESTER and BRISTOL.

TARTAN TIES

100% PURE WOOL HANDWOVEN
AUTHENTIC TARTANS

●   MADE IN SCOTLAND BY "LOCHCARRON"

We have in stock the following Tartan Ties—price 7/6 each (children's size 5/6)   ●   POST FREE IN THE U.K.

IN ANCIENT COLOURS ONLY

1. Abercrombie	48. Dundas	95. Louise	141. Mackinlay	188. Nicolson Ht.
2. Anderson	49. Dyce	96. Macalister	142. Mackinnon Red	189. Nisbet
3. Angus	50. Elliot	97. Macalpine	143. Mackinnon Ht.	190. Ogilvie of Airlie
4. Armstrong	51. Erskine	98. Macarthur	144. Maclachlan	191. Ogilvie Old and Rare
5. Austin	52. Farquharson	99. Macauley	145. Maclachlan Old	192. Ogilvie Ht.
6. Barclay Dress	53. Ferguson	100. Macbean	146. Maclaine of Lochbuie	193. Oliphant
7. Barclay Ht.	54. Fletcher	101. Macbeth	147. Maclaine Ht.	194. Ramsay
8. Black Watch	55. Fletcher of Dunans	102. MacCallum	148. Maclaren	195. Ramsay Blue
9. Black Watch Dress	56. Forbes	103. MacColl	149. Maclean of Duart	196. Rattray
10. Brodie Red	57. Forsyth	104. Macdiarmid	150. Maclean Ht.	197. Rob Roy
11. Brodie Ht.	58. Fraser Dress	105. Macdonald of Boisdale	151. Macleod Dress	198. Robertson Red
12. Bruce	59. Fraser Ht.	106. Macdonald Clan	152. Macleod of Harris	199. Robertson Ht.
13. Buchanan	60. Galbraith	107. Macdonald of Clanranald	153. Macmillan Dress	200. Rose Red
14. Burnett	61. Gillies	108. Macdonald Dress	154. Macmillan Ht.	201. Rose Ht.
15. Caledonia	62. Gordon Clan	109. Macdonald of Glengarry	155. Macmillan Old	202. Ross Dress
16. Cameron Clan	63. Gordon Dress	110. Macdonald of the Isles Red	156. Macnab	203. Ross Ht.
17. Cameron of Erracht	64. Gordon Old	111. Macdonald of the Isles Ht.	157. Macnaughton	204. Rothesay, Duke of
18. Cameron of Lochiel	65. Gow	112. Macdonald of the Isles Ht.	158. Macneil of Barra	205. Rothesay, Duke of, Ht.
19. Campbell Ancient	66. Graham of Menteith	(Old)	159. Macneil of Colonsay	206. Royal Canadian Air Force
20. Campbell of Argyll	67. Graham of Montrose	113. Macdonald of Kingsburgh	160. Macpherson	207. Russell
21. Campbell of Breadalbane	68. Grant	114. Macdonald of Sleat	161. Macpherson Dress	208. Ruthven
22. Campbell of Cawdor	69. Gunn	115. Macdonald of Staffa	162. Macpherson Ht.	209. Scott
23. Campbell Dress	70. Hamilton	116. Macdonell of Keppoch	163. Macphie	210. Scott Black/White
24. Campbell of Loudon	71. Hamilton Ht.	117. Macdougall	164. Macquarrie	211. Scott Green
25. Carmichael	72. Hay	118. Macduff	165. Macqueen	212. Scott Ht.
26. Carnegie	73. Henderson	119. Macduff Dress	166. Macrae	213. Seton
27. Chisholm	74. Home	120. Macduff Ht.	167. Macrae of Conchra	214. Shaw
28. Chisholm Ht.	75. Hope-Vere	121. Macewan	168. Macrae Ht.	215. Shepherd
29. Christie	76. Hunter	122. Macfarlane Black/White	169. Mactaggart	216. Sinclair Red
30. Clergy	77. Huntly	123. Macfarlane Clan	170. Mactavish and Thomson	217. Sinclair Ht.
31. Cockburn	78. Inglis	124. Macfarlane Ht.	171. Malcolm	218. Skene
32. Colquhoun	79. Inverness	125. Macgillivray	172. Marshall	219. Smith
33. Cranston	80. Jacobite	126. Macgregor	173. Matheson Dress	220. Stewart of Appin
34. Crawford	81. Johnstone	127. Macgregor Ht.	174. Matheson Ht.	221. Stewart of Appin Ht.
35. Culloden	82. Keith	128. Machardy	175. Maxwell	222. Stewart of Atholl
36. Cumming Red	83. Kennedy	129. Macinnes Red	176. Melville	223. Stewart Black
37. Cumming Ht.	84. Kerr	130. Macinnes Ht.	177. Menzies Green	224. Stewart of Bute
38. Cunningham	85. Kilgour	131. Macintosh Clan	178. Menzies Black/White	225. Stewart Dress
39. Dalziel	86. Lamont	132. Macintosh Ht.	179. Middleton	226. Stewart Ht.
40. Davidson Clan	87. Lauder	133. Macintyre	180. Montgomerie	227. Stewart Old
41. Davidson of Tulloch	88. Lennox	134. Macintyre of Glenorch	181. Morrison Clan	228. Stewart Royal
42. Douglas	89. Leslie Red	135. Macintyre Ht.	182. Mowat	229. Sutherland Old
43. Douglas Grey	90. Leslie Green	136. Macivor	183. Munro	230. Urquhart
44. Drummond of Perth	91. Lindsay	137. Mackay	184. Murray Clan	231. Urquhart Broad Red
45. Dunbar	92. Livingstone	138. Mackay Blue	185. Murray of Tullibardine	232. Wallace
46. Dunblane	93. Logan and Maclennan	139. Mackenzie	186. Napier	233. Watson
47. Duncan	94. Lorne	140. Mackenzie Dress	187. Nicolson	234. Wemyss

IN MODERN COLOURS ONLY

301. Austin	324. Grant	347. Macintosh Ht.	370. Robertson Red	393. Dalziel
302. Baird Ht.	325. Gunn	348. Macintyre Ht.	371. Robertson Ht.	394. Dunbar
303. Buchanan	326. Hamilton Ht.	349. Mackay	372. Ross Dress	395. Duncan
304. Cameron Clan	327. Hay	350. Mackenzie	373. Russell	396. Ferguson
305. Cameron of Erracht	328. Hay and Leith	351. Mackenzie Dress	374. Scott	397. Forbes
306. Cameron of Lochiel	329. Hunter	352. Mackinnon Red	375. Scott Green	398. Galloway Red
307. Campbell Ancient	330. Johnstone	353. Maclaren Clan	376. Scott Ht.	399. Galloway Ht.
308. Campbell of Argyll	331. Keith	354. Maclean of Duart	377. Sinclair Red	400. Graham of Montrose
309. Campbell of Breadalbane	332. Kerr	355. Macleod of Harris	378. Sinclair Ht.	401. Hamilton
310. Campbell of Cawdor	333. Lamont	356. Macpherson Clan	379. Stewart of Appin	402. Henderson
311. Campbell Dress	334. Leslie Green	357. Macqueen	380. Stewart Ht.	403. Kennedy
312. Chisholm	335. Lindsay	358. Macrae	381. Stewart, Prince Charles Edward	404. Leslie Red
313. Davidson Clan	336. Livingstone	359. Macrae Ht.	382. Stewart Royal	405. Logan and Maclennan
314. Douglas	337. Macbeth	360. Marshall	383. Stewart Victoria	406. Macauley
315. Drummond Clan	338. Macdonald Clan	361. Matheson Dress	384. Strathearn	407. Macdougall
316. Duchess of Kent	339. Macdonald Dress	362. Maxwell	385. Wallace	408. Maclachlan
317. Farquharson	340. Macduff Ht.	363. Menzies Green	386. Anderson	409. Macleod Dress
318. Fraser Dress	341. Macewan	364. Montgomerie	387. Blair	410. Macnaughton
319. Fraser Ht.	342. Macfarlane Clan	365. Morrison Clan	388. Black Watch	411. Morgan
320. Galbraith	343. Macfarlane Ht.	366. Munro	389. Colquhoun	412. Nicolson
321. Gordon Clan	344. Macgregor	367. Murray Clan	390. Crawford	413. Ramsay
322. Gordon Dress	345. Macinnes Red	368. Princess Elizabeth	391. Cumming Red	414. Rose Red
323. Graham of Menteith	346. Macintosh Clan	369. Princess Margaret Rose	392. Cunningham	415. Stewart Dress
				416. Sutherland Old

● **ADDITIONS TO THE RANGE**

1957

(IN MODERN COLOURS)

417. Armstrong	422. Elliot	427. MacCallum	432. Macmillan Old
418. Barclay Dress	423. Macalister	428. Macduff	433. Macnab
419. Brodie Red	424. Macalpine	429. Macintyre	434. Macphie
420. Bruce	425. Macarthur	430. Macivor	435. Shaw
421. Cockburn	426. Macbean	431. Maclaine of Lochbuie	436. Urquhart

● **ALSO AVAILABLE IN THE SAME MATERIAL:**   *Ht. signifies HUNTING*

Scarves, 11½″ × 54″: 13/6   Sashes, 9″ × 90″: 19/6

Squares, 36″ × 36″: 25/-   Stoles, 27″ × 72″: 38/6

ESTABLISHED 1904

W. J. MILNE LIMITED

ABERDEEN · SCOTLAND

TELEPHONE: 23950   TELEGRAMS: "GALLOWSES"

Nature's Masterpieces

can be instantly recognised—so can

HARRIS TWEED

A masterpiece of Man _and_ Nature

Look for the Harris Tweed Trade Mark. It is a Certification Mark and, as such, has been granted with the approval of the Board of Trade.

THE MARK warrants that the tweed to which it is applied is made from virgin Scottish wool, spun, dyed, hand-woven and finished IN THE OUTER HEBRIDES. _Beware of imitations._

THIS IS HOW
▼

LOOK FOR THIS MARK
ON THE CLOTH ▶

LOOK FOR THIS LABEL
◀ **ON THE GARMENT**

Issued by THE HARRIS TWEED ASSOCIATION LIMITED.

Scotland respects the gifted cook, and welcomes every technical improvement which advances her art.

M-m-m-m-m!

This welcome has been warmly extended to the new GAS cookers, which are designed to ensure consistently *good* cooking over many, many years.

Gas Cookers provide, for oven and hotplate, a more delicate gradation of heat than does any other type of cooker. They offer, among numerous other refinements, long-period automatic timers, eye-level grills, ovens to take a 26-lb turkey — and quite startling economy on the new cheaper Gas tariff.

Call at your Gas Service Centre and see the range of handsome Gas cookers.

SCOTTISH GAS

Eric Fraser

Motorised Banks for the Highlands & Islands

WORLD-WIDE INTEREST IN A NATIONAL BANK INNOVATION

UNTIL NOVEMBER 1946, whenever crofter weavers on Lewis and Harris were due for well-earned payments they had to make the journey — and for many of them it was an arduous one — to Stornoway, the tweed-manufacturing centre. But that was before the National Bank of Scotland decided that the time had come for banks, like foot battalions, to become motorised. Now, a ' lorried bank ', based on the Stornoway branch, brings banking service to all the scattered communities of Lewis and Harris.

From the first, this service proved so welcome that very soon other remote territories were enjoying its benefits. Since 1947 a second bank-on-wheels, based on Fort William, has operated regularly in the Onich, Strontian, Acharacle, Spean Bridge area. A third vehicle is based on Thurso, journeying twice a week to the Atomic Energy Authority's site at Dounreay where it becomes a temporary sub-branch. This service was introduced in 1955 and has proved very convenient for the employees of the Authority and for the construction firms working on the nuclear power station.

Other British banks have followed the National Bank's lead. They use (mostly) caravan-type mobile sub-branches, such as now attend so many of the important Agricultural Shows. But this type would be useless in the road conditions of the Isles and the N.W. Highlands, which demand a self-contained vehicle, rugged as the lovely country it traverses.

The National Bank's enterprise has aroused world-wide interest, resulting in many enquiries from abroad and visits from representatives of foreign banks.

To us, at the National Bank, it has been a source of satisfaction to have been the pioneers in this interesting, in fact rather romantic, field. To have been, if you will forgive the pun, literally, in the van. For there is nothing so good for morale as to be conscious of having made a little (beneficial) history.

THE NATIONAL BANK OF SCOTLAND LIMITED •

"...an' when I've been specially good I get something specially nice... McVitie & Price biscuits"

DIGESTIVE
Sweet Meal
BISCUITS
by

McVITIE & PRICE

Makers of Finest Quality Biscuits

MCVITIE & PRICE LTD · EDINBURGH   LONDON · MANCHESTER

12   xxxvii

INVERNESS — the home of *BURNETTS' Shortbread*

The sight of such a beautiful place as Inverness always conjures up memories of other good things—morning coffee, lunch or tea in Burnetts'—that friendly restaurant in the centre of the city—or the delight on a friend's face when opening a tin of Burnett's famous shortbread—the sort that is made with real butter only and is just perfect. Burnetts' shortbread is sent by post all over the world to folk who appreciate good things.

BURNETTS' OF INVERNESS
Academy St., Inverness   High St., Nairn

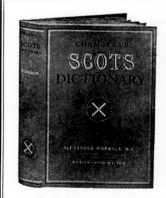
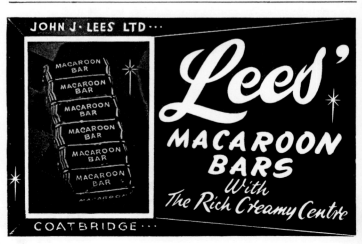

FOR SCOTS THE WORLD OVER

At the beginning of each month, thousands of copies of Scotland's Magazine start their various journeys from Scotland to all parts of the earth. To Scots and lovers of Scotland overseas they bring a little bit of Scotland, a breath of the heather-scented hills, pictures of well-kent places and faces, memories of past glories and news of Scotland's progress in the arts and sciences.

Nearly every one of you who reads this has a relation or an auld acquaintance overseas. What more kindly thought this year than to send as a present a year's subscription to Scotland's Magazine? The cost is only 25s. United Kingdom, ($3.27 in the U.S.A.) which covers packing and postage, 19s. 6d. ($2.77) to Canada and 23s. 6d. to other countries.

SCOTLAND'S MAGAZINE, 6-7 CASTLE TERRACE, EDINBURGH

fine and dandy . . .

PROCRASTINATION is the thief of tyre confidence. So why neglect to replace a
worn tyre until the last moment and leave that nagging little doubt in your mind that it
might let you down. Replace it with a trusted friend—Dunlop—and
everything will be fine. As to dandy, why, that little extra touch
of smartness—the Dunlop "White Sidewall"—is as good as a new bow
tie on a bright Sunday morning. There's a lot in it, you know—
this confidence in Dunlop!

DUNLOP *built better to last longer*

6H/133

TURNBERRY HOTEL

Ayrshire

The famous resort hotel on the warm and sheltered Ayrshire coast.
The championship Ailsa and Arran Golf Courses, Pitch and Putt Course, Tennis
Courts, Indoor Swimming Pool.

OPEN ALL THE YEAR

The Resident Manager will be happy to send full particulars – Telephone: Turnberry 202

BRITISH TRANSPORT HOTELS
for receptions, dances and all social occasions

Edinburgh: THE CALEDONIAN HOTEL – *Tel: Caledonian 2433* · Edinburgh: THE NORTH BRITISH HOTEL – *Tel: Waverley 2414*

Glasgow: THE ST. ENOCH HOTEL – *Tel: Central 7033* · Perth: THE STATION HOTEL – *Tel: Perth 741*

The Resident Managers will be happy to submit detailed quotations for any type of social function

BETTYHILL HOTEL
BETTYHILL · Sutherland
The Ideal Hotel for a Fishing Holiday
Good Food and every comfort. Excellent Sport on River and Lochs—Salmon, Sea Trout, Brown Trout. *Terms from Manageress*
'Grams—Hotel, Bettyhill · 'Phone—Bettyhill 202

CAPE WRATH HOTEL DURNESS Sutherlandshire
Situated amidst magnificent scenery overlooking the Kyle of Durness. Salmon and Sea Trout Fishing in River Dionard and Kyle of Durness. Brown Trout Fishing on Calladale, and eleven other lochs. Durness lochs are famous for their large Brown Trout.
Excellent Sea Bathing · Boating, Etc.
R.S.A.C. and A.A. · 'Phone No.—Durness 204

SCOTTISH CLAN CREST WALL PLAQUES

39/6
Plus 1/6 postage to all parts of the world

Made in Scotland

ANY CLAN OR TARTAN

TAYLORS ARTS
506 UNION STREET ABERDEEN

Scottish Tweed Patterns by Post

These lovely fabrics are fashioned for to-day in new patterns, colours and weights for men and women. We would like to send our samples, to be returned.

FRAZERS OF PERTH LTD.
Scottish Tweed House

THE HOUSE FOR TARTAN IN THE NORTH
If you have a Tartan we have it
STOCKISTS OF OVER 200 AUTHENTIC TARTANS
Orders and Enquiries Home and Overseas prompt service
R. S. MACDONALD & CO. LTD.,
**THE KILTMAKERS
56 EASTGATE, INVERNESS**

INDEX TO ADVERTISEMENTS

Hotels, Restaurants, etc.

Pictorial Acknowledgments

ON THE DUST COVER

J. Lamotte, colour photograph, outside dust cover.
Stephens Orr, inside dust cover.

SCOTLAND FOR THE BEGINNER

Scotland's Magazine, page 4 (top left).
Ian Gilchrist, page 4 (foot left).
J. Allan Cash, page 4 (foot centre).
J. C. H. Balmain, page 4 (foot right).
Photo Illustrations, page 5 (top).
Scotsman Publications Ltd., page 5 (foot right).

SCOTS AT SCHOOL

John Topham Ltd., page 6.
R. A. Laing, page 7.

SCOTS AT WORK

A. C. Browne, page 8 (top).
Fred. G. Sykes, page 8 (foot).
J. Lamotte, colour photograph, page 9.
Ian Craig, colour photograph, page 10.
G. W. Gibson, page 11 (top).
Scotland's Magazine, page 11 (foot) and page 14 (foot right).
Colvilles Ltd., page 12, page 14 (top and foot left), page 15, colour photograph, and page 16, colour photograph.
Quasi-Arc Limited, page 13.

THE WEARING OF THE KILT

Pictorial Press, page 17, page 18 (left and top right), page 19 (foot left and top right).
Scotland's Magazine, page 19 (top left and foot right).

SCOTS AT PLAY

P. Leddy, page 20 (top).
Scottish Daily Mail, page 20 (foot), page 21, page 22 (foot left) and page 28 (foot).
Recklaw Photos, page 22 (top left).
G. M. Cowie, page 22 (top right).
C. & F. McKean, page 22 (foot right).
Alan C. Browne, colour photograph, page 23.
A. Ronald Aitchison, colour photograph, page 24.
D. Phillips, page 25.
Alex. Tewnion, page 26.
B. H. Humble, page 27 (right).
Scotland's Magazine, page 28 (top), page 31 (centre right), page 32 (foot right).
David A. Lawrie, colour photograph, page 29.
Scotsman Publications Ltd., page 29 (foot).
John S. Logan, colour photograph, page 30.
Scottish Youth Hostels Association, page 31 (top left and right and foot right).
J. H. Cuthill, page 32 (top).
Star Photos, Perth, page 32 (foot left), page 33 (top right).
A. G. Ingram, page 32 (centre right).
Alex. C. Cowper, page 33 (top left).
John Atkinson, page 33 (foot).
Aberdeen Journals Ltd., page 34 (top).
John G. Wilson, page 34 (foot).
The British Travel and Holidays Association, colour photograph, page 35.

LIFE IN THE HIGHLANDS

W. A. Poucher, colour photograph, page 36.
W. Gordon Smith, page 37 (top).
J. Allan Cash, page 37 (foot), page 38, page 39, page 44.

A. P. Bennett, sketch, page 40.
J. Lamotte, colour photograph, page 41.
David A. Lawrie, colour photograph, page 42.
Valentine & Sons Ltd., page 43 (top).
Mabel H. Lowe, page 43 (foot).
North of Scotland Hydro Electric Board, page 45 (top).
Scotland's Magazine, page 45 (foot).

SCOTLAND'S STATISTICAL ACCOUNT

J. Telfer Dunbar, page 46.
Portrait of Sir John Sinclair of Ulbster reproduced by permission of the Viscount Thurso, and colour blocks loaned by The Medici Society Ltd., London, page 47.
Tom Weir, colour photograph, page 48.
J. Allan Cash, page 48 (foot).
P. K. McLaren, page 49, and page 50.
Basil Gibsone, page 51 (top right).

DESIGN IN SCOTLAND

Alf Daniel, page 52 (top left).
Annan of Glasgow, page 52 (foot).
J. Lamotte, page 53 (top).
The British Travel and Holidays Association, page 53 (foot), page 55 (top left).
B. G. Allan, page 54 (top left).
Coopey of Aberdeen, page 54 (top right) and page 60 (top).
The Council of Industrial Design, Scottish Committee, page 54 (foot), page 56, page 59 (top).
Hans Wild photographs by permission of Hogg of Hawick, page 55 (top right), and colour photograph, page 57.
Scotland's Magazine, page 55 (foot), page 58 (top right and left, foot right and left).
Ideal Studios, page 58 (centre right, left and centre).
H. Morris and Co. Ltd., page 59 (foot).
Iain Cameron-Taylor, page 60 (foot left).
John Mackay, page 60 (foot right).
Caithness Brothers, page 61.

SCOTS AT TABLE

Scotland's Magazine, page 62, page 65, page 66 and page 67.
Violet Banks, page 63 and page 64 (foot left).
The British Travel and Holidays Association, page 64 (centre and top left).
Scottish Tourist Board, page 64 (foot right).

SCOTS AT WAR

Scotland's Magazine, page 68, page 69.
Painting by Colonel O. E. B. MacLeod, page 70.
John Mackay, page 71 and page 73 (foot).
Army Public Relations, page 72.
Imperial War Museum, Crown Copyright, page 73 (top).

THE WATER OF LIFE

Pictorial Press, page 74 and page 75.

SCOTS AND THEIR MUSIC

Scotland's Magazine, colour photograph, page 76, page 77 and page 78.
The British Travel and Holidays Association, page 79.
Norward Inglis for *Scotland's Magazine*, colour photograph, page 80 (top).
Scotsman Publications Ltd., page 80 (foot).

The publishers would like to acknowledge with gratitude the courteous co-operation received from Messrs. Colvilles Ltd. during preparation of this publication.

PRINTED IN SCOTLAND BY J. AND J. GRAY, ANNANDALE STREET, EDINBURGH